Hit On The Head With A Sledgehammer : A Written Mix Tape

Steve Baba

Crimson Milk Press
San Francisco

Copyright © 2015 Steve Baba

Cover design by Steve Baba

Ways to contact the author:
www.stevebaba.com
facebook.com/stevebaba
twitter.com/stevenhbaba

First printing, April 2015
Printed in the USA

ISBN: 0692404031
ISBN-13: 978-0692404034

Table Of Contents

Short Stories And Essays

For Cariss Gorman- a shining light in my life. May your light never dim.

Short Stories And Essays

Yosemite

I must be insane, I thought to myself, climbing ever so slowly.
The heat was washing over my body like waves of invisible fire.
Each wave that passed through me would extract just a little more
energy, a little more moisture that was essential to my body's
functioning. My leather booted feet placed one in front of the
other on the granite sand path. The angle upwards seemed to be at
forty-five degrees. All I had was a small rucksack, and that even
felt like a ton of bricks. Even the pine trees that stood on each
side of the path were against me, their branches graciously
parting so the scorching rays of Apollo could strike me. A single
wasp found me. It buzzed around my head, circling at an
aggravating and fearful speed. Great, I'm going to get stung as
well.

Yosemite Valley is located about 4 hours east from San Jose,
California. It is firmly placed in the Sierra Nevada Mountains,
which are in Central California. Yosemite has been known for its
ancient granite and the famed Half Dome, an icon for the national
park. It boasts millions of visitors a year and is world famous.
Abundant with natural wonders such as the granite monolith El
Capitan and Yosemite Falls, it is a testament to the memory of
John Muir, a naturalist who had a great fondness of the valley. I
have my own fondness to this place, as it is almost like a home to
me. Each and every time I come to Yosemite, it is like stepping
through a doorway and entering another world. It brings me peace
and I feel not only refreshed but at ease. My time has been spent
in Yosemite hiking its steep, dangerous trails that lead to
spectacular views from above the valley. And this time, I may
have pushed my luck.

I had already gone up the dreaded granite steps of Vernal
Falls. These steps come in sizes two and three feet and if you are
as short as I am, they can be leg busters. By the way, I'm 5'4. The
steps go up the right side of the falls, seemingly right next to the

clear rush of water that pummels the rocks below. If you are lucky enough to still have your legs when you reach the top, then you truly are in great shape. Then it is off to Nevada Falls, a bit higher and more into the valley. Though not as strenuous as Vernal, the trail that leads to the top of the falls is narrow and sometimes can be blocked by melting snow packs. Sure, you can walk or climb over these snow packs, but the drop to the left of you is down. Straight down and very steep. After the passing of Nevada Falls, you go into this lightly forested dirt path. It leads into a smaller valley, aptly named Little Yosemite Valley. There is a small campground and limited facilities. It is after passing this, you are getting into the backcountry.

I took a deep breath and the air sizzled my lungs. I had to take out a small hand towel to wipe the sweat from my eyes. At the moment they burned and I was stupid enough to rub them, which made them burn even more. Tears formed and I was temporarily blinded. With the loud buzz of the wasp still present, I swatted into the air with my hands vigorously, hoping the wasp would give up on stinging me. I heard a couple of quick buzzes around my left ear, and then silence. Oh shit. Did he land on me, getting ready to puncture me? Or did he finally get the damn message that he had annoyed me quite enough? I blinked once and my vision returned, albeit a bit blurry, like when you first spray the windshield with the clear fluid and all it does is smear the dirt all around the glass instead of wiping it off. I could focus a little more clearly, and there I was. The path in front of me, still going straight up to the sky. The pines standing tall on each side of the path, dark green and silent. And the ever present 104 degree temperature. But no buzz. Aha!

I decided to stop and relish in my victory over the wasp, and sat on a rather large granite rock. It was unusually flat with granite dust on it. I took off my rucksack and took out a bottle of warm water. I could have sworn that the bottle was ice cold when I left for the hike in the early morning. With myself refueling and resting, I took notice of the silence. It was really, really quiet. No birds singing, no rustling of the pine trees' branches, nothing. It was as if time had stopped and I was living in a vacuum. The sky was a beautiful azure blue with not a cotton ball in sight. I moved my foot slightly and it seemed to be amplified, the sound being at volume level 8 instead of the normal 2. There wasn't a soul around. I had finally gotten away from my angst ridden civilization mentality. I sniffed the air. Not a touch or hint of human created toxic fumes. Just pure clean wilderness oxygen. My God, I should move out here.

Hiking has always been a great interest to me. Not only a hobby but more close to a mentality. Perhaps a nomadic, wandering mentality that has always been a part of myself since I was young. Hiking has always been a pleasure for me, even though it may be body wracking, muscle aching and joint tweaking. An inner peace, to be with one's own thoughts and actually expand your frame of mind, away from the hindrances of modern civilized life. We hide in our little worlds, behind cubicles and television screens. Listening to what is right, what is wrong and how one must go about being successful in the society and civilization we as humans have created for ourselves. I'd rather go hiking. And the places I've hiked have been nothing less than pure natural beauty. It's better looking at the wilderness instead of a block of buildings any day.

Refreshed but still baking like a shake and bake chicken, I stood up and felt my legs go wobbly. Was I that out of shape? I looked down and saw that I had stepped onto a loose branch. The heat was getting to me, I thought. I kicked the branch aside and started to move up the trail. My legs still felt like jelly, so I bent over and reached for my feet. My hamstrings immediately tensed. Sharp pains shot through each leg. I growled and sat on the trail. They were cramping up. I grabbed my left foot and pulled it up into the air. The sharp twisting pain slowly went away as the hamstring straightened out. But while I was working on my left hamstring, the other one was seizing quite strongly, and it hurt like a mother. I quickly released the left foot as soon as the cramp worked itself out and immediately reached for my right foot, desperate to stop the pain that was almost making my eyes roll into their sockets. Instant relief in a matter of seconds as I pulled hard on my boot toe. Cramps must be one of the worst pains one has to endure, except when one gets hit point blank by a baseball in the jaw.

I felt a little better, the legs stretched out. I started to walk again. The trail was dusty, and for each step I took, the dust kicked up. Luckily there was a wind and the dust was being blown behind me. I took each step slowly. The trail was adorned with pine trees that bended overhead. I took a breath of air. It was hot, but it felt good in my lungs.

As I made my way up the trail, I noticed little things. The rays of sun poking through the pines, a squirrel that scampered across the trail, and some birds that flew from branch to branch. I felt at peace and I knew that nature was something I needed in my life more than ever at the moment.

I was on my way to a larger destination that would, I hope, take my breath away. I trudged on for an hour, and the environment didn't change. Then there was a turn in the trail, and it led to an opening where there were some huge rock outcroppings. I was pretty sure that they were granite. I stood on one of them as I caught my breath. The sun was blazing, and I felt like I was going to turn into a raisin. There was a sign nearby, and it said my destination was about a half mile away.

The rest of the trail was open. There weren't any trees. Just the dust of the trail and some granite rocks on the sides of the trail. I was feeling a little lightheaded. After I hiked the ½ mile, I came upon a curved mountain. That was my destination. I went up it. It wasn't steep or slippery. I made it to the top. There was room for only one person. I looked at the benchmark and it said Cloud's Rest, 9,931 feet. I was so happy, that I forgot that I was on such a small space, and jumped up into the air. I almost fell off, and the sweat on my brow bled into my eyes. I wiped it away. Then I saw two people coming from the other side of Cloud's Rest. They were a couple of women. I said hello to them. They were out of breath, and just waved to me. I looked at the valley view, and it was stunning. I saw all the little pine trees in the valley. I also saw the Merced River that cut through the valley. I sat down and took an apple out from my backpack. I nibbled on it and breathed deeply. The women didn't stay long. They went back from where they came from. So there I was, all alone, on top of a wonderful scene.

I saw Half Dome. It looked like when you saw it from the valley floor, but this view was from the side. It looked majestic. I sat there for a few minutes. Then it was back to the trail. It was pretty easy getting back to the junction, though my knees felt it since it was mostly downhill. The sun was still shining hot. I hiked up the left trail and went up and up. There were people mostly coming down. I tried to say hi to everyone, but there were too many. So I just nodded when I saw someone coming down the trail.

I made it up to The Steps To Hell, which were the steps that led up to the curve of Half Dome. They were strenuous, and I felt it in my legs. There were people going up and down. I just concentrated on the steps, as they were about a 1/3 of a height of my own body. They weren't straight. They were cut at rough angles, and some were higher on the left side than the right side. Also some with a higher right side than the left. It took me a half hour to get past this point. I made it to the cables. The cables were the last part of getting to the top of Half Dome. I took my time. I had some really good hiking boots, and they stuck to the granite. I had to wait every so often, as people were also climbing it, albeit gingerly. I felt happy and confident. This was my 2nd time up this glorious piece of rock.

I finally made it to the top. There were a few people here, more than Cloud's Rest. There was a couple standing near me arguing. I interrupted them and asked if they could take a picture of me at the Diving Board. The Diving Board was a piece of rock that stuck out into the void and you could get a really good picture of someone on it. It looked like you were suspended in the air. The man of the couple took the camera. I adjusted my hat and sunglasses and stood out on the Diving Board. He waved to me after he took the picture. I thanked him and said I would do the same, if they wanted it. They agreed, and went out on the Diving Board. I took their picture. When the man came back to retrieve his camera, he threw up. I was concerned. I gave him some water and the woman thanked me. He said he felt better. I told them I would follow them down to the junction to make sure they were alright.

I looked at the valley floor. Somewhere, down there, was my campsite and my friends. I looked at it for a while, then checked on the couple. The guy looked better, but I wanted to make sure they were okay. The sun was getting lower. I hoped to make it to the valley floor before it got dark. If not, I was in trouble. I didn't have a flashlight, and it would be pitch dark.

We went down the cables. I glided down without trouble. Then the steps, which were easier coming down than going up. We went down the trail and got to the junction. The sun was even lower, and I knew that it would be way past dark when I got back to the valley floor. We passed Little Yosemite Valley and the couple decided to stay there for the night. I said my goodbyes and kept on going. In 10 minutes it was dark. I was in deep trouble. I couldn't see my hands in front of my face. I had to decide; get off to the side of the trail and sleep, or go back to Little Yosemite. Just as I was making my decision, I saw a light.

It was a couple of men and their sons. They asked me where I was going, and I told them I would like to make it to the valley floor. They said I could hitch a ride with them. I was instantly relieved. My steps were heavy, as I didn't know where they were stepping. We made it to Nevada Falls, and then it was down the steps. I stumbled quite a lot and almost fell, but the group was still there, and I was grateful that they were there.

The pace we were going down was quick. I was sweating profusely. We made it down to the valley floor. I could see campsite lights and fires. I thanked my new found friends and groped through the almost dark to my campsite.

My friend was cooking noodles as I came up to our campsite. He greeted me and asked if I was okay. He thought that I was going to be stranded up in the mountains and that I would come down in the morning. I laughed nervously and said I found a group of night hikers that let me follow them down the trails to the valley floor. I took off my shirt. It was drenched. I drank a lot of water and finished a liter bottle. Then, as I cooled down, I sat down at the table and got ready to eat.

The Will

He died at 4:32 am on a Tuesday morning. He was alone. He was always alone. He didn't like people. He had no friends. Estranged from family. But he had a soft spot for his sister. They were close as children, and close as adults. That is until, of course, when she married. He hated her husband. He was angry because her husband was a controlling misogynist. So reluctantly he cut off his ties with his sister. When he got ill, he didn't tell anyone. Cancer. When he was on his last leg, he told the executor of his will to sign her as the owner of all and everything he had.

She learned of the news a couple of days ago. He died in his sleep, she was told. As she wiped tears from her eyes, she recalled the day when he didn't show up at her wedding. It made her especially sad because that day was supposed to be the happiest of all days. The chair he was supposed to sit on was empty. She looked at it many times before she said her vows.

Now he was gone, and she wouldn't see him alive ever again. She told her husband and his face was grim. They sat in the living room and sipped tea in silence. Finally she got up to use the bathroom.

She called the rest of the family. They were just as sad as her, and they asked her if she was okay. She replied that she was tough and that she would get through it. She called her best friend Lacey. She was always ready to listen when she had a problem or was going through something with her husband. She told Lacey that her brother had died. Lacey gasped as she tightly held onto the receiver. She started to talk about their childhood. How they would go down to the creek near their childhood home and throw rocks into it. Then she told Lacey the time when he stuck up for her in school when someone called her a nigger. He fought tooth and nail with those white boys, and in the end he ended up beaten and bruised. But they never called her that name again.

She reminisced about other things. Like the time when she was stuck in a barrel. If her parents had found out, she would have been spanked for sure. He got her out of it smoothly. And they kept it a secret between them. And then the boy whom she was dating in high school. He was there when her boyfriend slapped her for being late on a date. He punched him in the nose, and broke it. Tears were coming down her cheeks as she told Lacey these things. She told Lacey that she hadn't talked to him in 20 years. Her 20 year wedding anniversary was coming up. Lacey told her to be strong and that she would be there for her.

A couple of days later, and the phone rang. Her husband answered it. He listened intently to the voice on the other line. He wrote some notes on a piece of paper and then thanked the caller. He went to find her and she was in bed looking at old photographs of she and her brother. She looked up when he entered the room.

"It was the executor. He says he's going to read the will in a couple days. You know he was rich, Darla. I wonder where all that cash is going to wind up?"

"Ted. Don't worry about that. Money isn't everything."

"Yeah, but he was rich! You know what we could do with that money?"

Darla frowned and put down the photograph book. She thought about why Ted would be so concerned about money. They had enough coming in with his job at the tech company. She worked as a substitute teacher when they needed extra cash.

She thought of the time when she was locked out of the house and Jim pulled her through the open window of his bedroom. She was as scared as a mouse, but Jim made her feel better. She started to cry again, but silently so Ted didn't notice.

The day of the will reading came fast. As Darla and Jim were the only ones listed on the will envelope, they were the only ones there to hear what the executor was going to say. The room was small, and had books lined on each wall. A small wood desk was near a window, and Darla and Ted sat near the desk. The executor was sitting behind the desk, with the envelope in his hand.

"Let's get to it, shall we?" the executor said. Both of them nodded.

He opened the envelope and took out a piece of parchment. It was yellowed and it seemed to have come from the 19th century. The executor smoothed out the parchment and started to read aloud.

"I, Jim Abernathy, Of sound mind and body…..bequeath my whole fortune and belongings to Darla Quinn. When this will is read, she will take total control of my assets. As of this written statement I am worth 3 million dollars. This shall be immediately transferred to Darla Quinn."

Darla sat there stunned. She didn't know her brother had amassed a fortune as big as 3 million dollars. She looked at Ted. He was smirking. She didn't know what that meant, but she kept calm enough to talk to the executor.

"When will the transfer take place?" she asked.

"Tomorrow, at noon. Please supply me with your bank account number and bank. I'll make sure there is no trouble with this transaction."

She shook the hand of the executor and followed her husband out the door. They got into their beat up Ford Taurus and sat there silently for a few minutes. Then Ted spoke.

"Wow. 3 million smackeroos. We can do a lot with that!"

Darla closed her eyes. In her mind, her wish was to use the money to have Jim come back to life.

"It doesn't matter how much we got. We'll make a rational decision in the coming days. Until then, you have no right to touch that money. It's mine."

"But it's a joint account, honey. I have full access and that's that."

Darla frowned. She wagged a finger at Ted, but that was all.

"Please drop me off at Lacey's. I promised to see her after the reading of the will."

"Well, don't go blabbing to everyone that we got that much money. We'll have a line of people in front of our front door asking for something."

Darla sighed. She knew in her heart that Ted was a money grabbing fool. He would probably use the money to buy a new house, a new car, and gamble the rest away. But she trusted him enough to not touch the money at the moment.

Ted dropped Darla off at Lacey's. Darla knocked on the door and it opened a few seconds later. A middle aged woman with graying long blonde hair opened the door. It was Lacey. Lacey looked left and then right. She waited for Ted to pull away. When the coast was clear, she kissed Darla passionately on the mouth. Then she let her in. They embraced, and as Lacey had her arms tight around Darla, she felt her bare shoulder getting wet. Darla was crying. Lacey stroked Darla's short black hair. They let go of each other and then sat opposite one another on the couch.

"So sorry that you had to endure this, Darla."

"It's okay. Things could be worse."

"So, Ted doesn't know anything about us, right?"

"Yes, yes. He's as clueless as ever. All he wants is the damn money from Jim."

Lacey sighed. She placed her hand on Darla's thigh. She wondered what she would get out of this new development. Lacey wasn't poor, but she was always living from paycheck to paycheck. An infusion of money would make her life a whole lot easier. But she was more concerned with Darla. She hadn't seen her in 3 weeks, and she was getting horny.

But she knew anything outside of helping her through her grief was not going to happen. Lacey went to the kitchen and put on a pot of coffee. She got out the cookies that Darla liked, and put them on a plate. With the coffee made, she took out a tray and put two cups, the coffee pot and the cookies on it. She went back to the living room. Darla was staring into space, with a sad face.

"Here you go, my dear," said Lacey. She poured the coffee into each cup and handed a cookie to Darla.

"I don't trust him. I really don't. For the past few months, some money has been missing from the account. I don't know where it went, but I know I haven't spent it. I think he's taking out the money for something. He hasn't been to Gambler's Anonymous for a year now. If he's spending the money for gambling, I'm going to leave him."

Lacey sighed a sigh of relief. It would be good to have Darla here in her home. She was concerned what would happen to the money if she did indeed divorce. Darla took a sip of her coffee and laid back into the couch. Lacey kissed her on the cheek and she was visibly more relaxed now.

"So what are you going to do with the money? Maybe you could put it into one of those secret accounts in Switzerland or something."

Darla seemed lost in thought and didn't answer Lacey's question. Lacey made a mental note in her head to not talk about the money right now.

Darla went back home. Ted was waiting for her at the front door.

A twist in his stomach came and went. He was thinking about the money. He already knew how he was going to spend it.

Darla took a shower and then went into the kitchen. She made a pot roast with new potatoes and asparagus tips. As they ate in silence at the dinner table, Ted looked sidewise at Darla.

"Honey, about the money-"

Darla frowned and dropped her fork on her plate loudly.

"Yeah, so what about the money, Ted?"

"Well, we don't have to talk about it now. Let's finish dinner and watch a movie."

"Yes, let's not talk about it now."

Darla cleared the table and put the leftovers into the refrigerator. She went to the living room. Ted was just inserting the DVD into the player. The movie came on and they sat there on opposite sides of the couch watching it.

Why Jim? Why didn't you tell me? I wish you were here. Why did you give me all of that goddam money? You have made it worse for me and Ted. Damn you.

They went to bed. After the lights were turned out, each went to their part of the bed. Then Ted rolled over to Darla's side of the bed. He faced her back. He attempted to hold her from behind and cuddle, but she flinched at the first touch of his arm on her side. He rolled back to his side of the bed and closed his eyes.

When Darla woke up the next morning, Ted was gone. She looked at the alarm clock. It read eight-thirty. She went to the bathroom and went into the kitchen. There were dirty dishes in the sink. Ted had had an early breakfast. There was still fresh coffee in the coffee maker, so Darla poured herself a cup. She noticed an open envelope on the dining room table. There was no markings, except for their address, with an attention to Darla. Darla frowned and inspected the envelope. Nothing. She threw the envelope away and sighed. Soon tears were flowing down her face. She missed Jim. She remembered when Jim would come in late from drinking with his friends. If their father had known Jim was drinking, he would have been furious. So Darla would let him sleep on the floor of her bedroom.

The phone rang. Darla answered it on the 4th ring. It was the bank. They asked if she had just withdrawn 5,000 dollars from her account. Darla frowned when she heard this, and her first thought was that Ted took it. She said that yes, she indeed withdrew the money, and the bank wanted to verify it. Darla hung up the phone and started to weep.

She got into the car, with puffy red eyes and red face. She drove to Lacey's. When she got to Lacey's house, she frantically knocked on the door. Lacey, who had just woken up, opened the door in her sky blue robe and blonde hair tied up on her head. Darla embraced her and she said she wanted to be with her.

The smoke was thick in the air as Darla slept soundly next to Lacey. Lacey put out the cigarette and she thought that she was going to be able to have Darla for the rest of her life.

Crazy

Walk. Walk fast. Here comes someone. Look down. Don't make eye contact. Keep walking. The sun feels good on my face. Walk. Keep walking.

He was going to the store. He only went once a week, but that was enough. He was getting groceries. At a new place. He never went anywhere he had never been before, but his beloved store had discontinued the bar soap he bought. So he asked around and his neighbor suggested this store he was going to now. He was afraid. To look at anyone. To be in public. But how was he supposed to take a shower without his chosen soap?

We're almost there. Almost there. Don't think. Just walk. Walk quickly. Oh, here comes a mother with her stroller. Don't look at her. Keep quiet.

He made it to the store in 5 minutes. He didn't know the store was so close to him. How had he not known that it was that near? He went inside and quickly shuffled from aisle to aisle. There, in the 2nd row, was his soap. He bought 10 of them and then went to the checkout stand.

"Hello, how are you today?"

He looked down and nodded. He didn't realize that the checkout girl was gorgeous. She had medium length blonde hair, brown eyes and full red lips.

"Wow, I've never seen anyone buy so much of the same soap!"

He nodded and adjusted his glasses. She asked how he would like to pay, and he took out a few bills from his wallet. She rang up the sale and gave him back his change.

"Have a nice day."

He nodded, with his eyes averted, and quickly walked out of the store. He made it back to his apartment and locked up the door with its 5 locks. He sat down on the green couch and sighed a sigh of relief. Now that wasn't so bad, was it? He thought to himself. He put the bag of soap on the ground and took off his glasses. He turned on the television, and Judge Judy was on. He watched the full episode, and then went to the kitchen to make lunch. He put peanut butter on some wheat bread, then some grape jelly on another piece of bread. He poured himself a glass of milk and sat at the dining room table. As he ate, he read the newspaper. Not the NY Times or the Washington Post, but The National Enquirer. He loved tabloids. When he went to London, way before he was diagnosed, he read all the tabloids there. He remembered the Page 3 girl, and how he would blush as he stared at a half-naked woman, her massive breasts covering the newsprint.

He went on the computer. He opened the chat screen and saw that 3 of his friends were online. He clicked on one of his friend's icons and waited. It was Jim. The chat screen opened and Jim was typing a message. Hey- how's it going? Jim asked. Not bad, not bad at all, he replied. They chatted for a while, and when he got bored, he signed off.

He made his dinner of rice and chicken. Made the same way, every time. He ate in front of the television, watching The Big Bang Theory. He loved that sitcom. He finished his dinner and then washed the dishes. He finished the dishes and then went to take a shower. He always took a shower in the evening so he would feel clean when he went to bed. After taking a shower he brushed his teeth. As he tried to apply the toothpaste to his toothbrush, nothing came out. Damn! I need toothpaste! That meant that he had to go out in public again. His heart started to race, and he sat down at his desk to make a note to get toothpaste tomorrow.

By the time he got to the bedroom, he had calmed down. He put on his pajamas and pulled the blankets back to get in. Then he pulled the blankets to his chest and turned out the light. He slept well. Usually he woke every two to three hours, but this night he slept all the way through. Eight hours straight.

He got up around 7 am, and went to the bathroom. After that he went into the kitchen to make tea. He used to drink coffee, but it would affect his bowels badly. So it was English Breakfast tea. The water boiled and he put a packet of tea into his favorite mug, that said, "Don't Quit", on it. He poured the hot water into the mug and waited about 5 minutes. Then he took out the teabag and squeezed the lingering hot water from it and into the mug. He added two scoops of sugar and stirred it. First, a light sip. Ah, it was hot. Then a little more. Better. Delicious. Nothing like tea in the morning. He went to the kitchen cabinet and took out a loaf of wheat bread. He took out two slices and put them into the toaster. He got the butter out of the refrigerator while the bread toasted. Then when the toast sprang up, he gingerly held them and put them on a porcelain plate. It was blue, his favorite color. He buttered the toast and took it to the living room.

He turned on the television and watched the morning news. Nothing worth thinking about, he thought to himself. Then he put in a DVD of Scooby Doo, and as he watched the cartoon, he nibbled on the toast. He sipped from the mug, and in between sips, he would laugh out loud from watching the cartoon.

After breakfast, he turned off the television and turned on the laptop. He waited as it booted up. Then when the laptop was fully operational, he checked his email. He had one from his mom. She wanted to know if he was alright. He had forgotten to call her yesterday. He made note and stuck it to the screen with the words, "Call Mom", on it. Another email from his friend in Mexico. She was traveling with her family to sightsee and she was his best friend. They hadn't seen each other in 2 years, since she moved to Boston to go to college.

He looked at the clock on the wall : 10:00 am. Well, I guess I'd better go get that toothpaste. He shivered slightly, and his face started to burn. His heartbeat raced and he thought he was going to perspire. He closed his eyes as the fear started to creep into his body. He breathed slowly, from nose to mouth. After a few minutes, he was calmer. He wasn't calm, but calmer.

He put on a pair of jeans, that were brand new, a black long sleeve t-shirt, and he put on his always reliable sneakers. The rubber on the bottom of those sneakers were coming off. He didn't dare go into a shoe store.

He turned all the locks on the door off, and took a cautionary step outside. Nobody there. Good. He exited his apartment and locked the door. He walked quickly down the stairs to the awaiting sunshine. When he exited the apartment complex, he took a deep breath and walked forward.

Look down. Yes, look down. Am I sweating? No, I don't think so. Put one foot in front of the other. There you go. Yes, one-two, one-two. There's a man coming. I see him. He's wearing a yellow raincoat. Why is he wearing a yellow raincoat? Don't think. Just go. Yes, just go. Damn! I forgot to turn off the computer. Can't go back now. Yes, let the man with the yellow raincoat pass first. There. Finished. Keep walking. There's the entrance. Go, go, go.

He entered the store and felt flushed. He was worried people thought he was on drugs, so he kept his search for the toothpaste at a minimum. He, with a lot of trouble, found the aisle with the toothpaste. Luckily, the store was almost empty, so he wasn't on the verge of going crazy. He found the right size and flavor of his brand of toothpaste, and his heart dropped to his stomach, as he had to interact with another human to buy his toothpaste.

He went to the checkout stand and the same girl was there to check him out. He looked down as he handed the toothpaste to her.

"Hi! It's me. You remember me, right?"

No answer. His face getting even more red. She sensed something wrong and put her hand on his.

"Hey, it's okay. Don't worry. You'll be okay. How are you today?"

"Um, fine."

"So you do talk! Hi, my name is April. What's yours?"

"Um, Dave."

"Nice to meet you Dave!'

No answer.

"Well, here's your toothpaste. Have a nice day!"

Dave took the bag and went outside. He looked at his hand gingerly. Was it hurt? Were there any marks? He felt his heart slowing, and the usual pale cheeks were coming back to him. He walked back, still looking down, but with a skip to his step.

Dave went into his apartment and locked the door. He was smiling. He felt light. He felt so good. He went to the bathroom to brush his teeth. Then he made lunch. The rest of the day was mellow and easy for him.

He wanted to go back to the market. But he didn't have anything to buy. He could buy food. He could stock up on canned goods. So he decided to go.

Walk. Walk slowly. Try to look up. The sun feels so good today. There's the mailman. I think he's a good person. Ah.

Dave entered the market and got a shopping cart. He went to the canned goods section and bought many cans of vegetables. Then soup. And finally canned fruit. He secretly hoped that she would be there to check him out.

As Dave was going to the checkout stand, he felt his heart pounding. Not like before. This time there wasn't the threat of death. But of hope.

She was at the same checkout stand as before, and she saw Dave. Dave, with his head up, took his first look at her. He thought she was perfect. He half-smiled and put his canned goods on the conveyor belt.

"Hey there, how are you today?" she asked.

"Pretty good, I guess."

"Wow, that's a lot of canned goods! You must be stocking up!"

"Yup."

She rang up all the cans and put them into some plastic bags.

"Don't be a stranger!" she told Dave.

Dave smiled and took his groceries.

When Dave got back to the apartment, he put his key into the door knob lock. As he did this, the door opened slightly, before Dave could turn the lock. I forgot to lock the door! Damn! What the hell is wrong with me? Dave entered the apartment and closed the door with a slam. He double-checked each lock to make sure they were locked. Dave started to sweat, and his chest was constricting. He sat down with a glass of orange juice. Soon the anxiety passed and he relaxed.

Dave relaxed the rest of the day. He made a peanut butter and jelly sandwich for lunch and he put away his canned goods. He watched television for a little while, but he found that he couldn't concentrate. He was thinking about her. He was thinking about April. She was so kind. She was a good person. And she was beautiful.

Dave spent the evening reading. He was reading The Year Of Fog by Michelle Richmond. It was pretty good. That was the only thing he could do to take his mind off of April. He made a dinner of steak and potatoes, and continued to read until late. He made a chamomile tea and went to bed.

He got up early, before the alarm went off. He felt good. Really good. There was a warmth coming from his chest that he never felt before. He got up, went to the bathroom and then went to the kitchen to make his tea. He thought about what he would do today. He knew he had to go back to the market, but how would he justify what to buy? Dave bumped the bag of sugar and it fell to the ground with a thump. The whole bag emptied onto the floor. Oh, I think I need a bag of sugar! He said to himself.

Dave got dressed and went outside.

What a wonderful day! Here comes my neighbor. I'm going to say hi to him. Hi! The ground is so dirty. Why was I looking at it all the time? Let the breeze flow through my hair. Feel the sunshine on my face. Oh, there's a poster with a baby on it. How cute!

Dave recognized after he entered the market that he had walked a whole 5 minutes slower to the market than he had previously. He took a basket and looked for the sugar. He found it. Then he walked around, milling around the various shoppers. Satisfied with being around people, he went to the checkout stand.

April was standing there staring into space. She had a slight smile on her face. When Dave came up to her, she smiled brightly.

"Hey there! How are you?" she said.

"Good, good."

"So sugar, huh? You must drink a lot of tea."

"How did you know?"

"I know these things, Dave."

"Ah."

"So, um, I was wondering, would you like to meet for a cup of coffee after my shift today?"

"Sure!"

"Okay, I get off at 4, so meet me in front of the store."

"Okay. See you then."

Dave saw in her eyes a brightness that he had only seen in movies. Dave took his sugar and went outside. Dave breathed in a deep breath of fresh air. Then he walked back to his apartment.

Smoking

I started smoking at 40 years old. I lived in New York City
and was having the time of my life. I met some new friends, went
to Manhattan and drank a lot of coffee. We used to drink on the
weekends and I would sit there on the front porch while my
friends smoked. But for some reason, even though I didn't smoke,
I wanted to. So I would ask for a cigarette with a bottle of beer in
my hand. The smoke made me feel good. I felt relaxed and really
liked it. I would ask for another cigarette and smoke it slowly.

Injoon was from Korea. He was in NYC to study English.
Kelly was a pilot for a small time airlines. Mathieu was from
France and he was working at an internship for a fashion
company. These were my friends at my house in Queens. They
were great and I enjoyed talking and hanging out with them.
Injoon smoked about 10 cigarettes a day. Kelly smoked when he
was drinking. Just like me.

Marlboro reds were our favorites. After smoking on the porch
while drinking, I thought it would be great smoking all the time.
The nicotine high was nice. It made things easier for me. We
smoked cigars too, but it wasn't the same as the cigarettes. Soon I
was buying a pack for myself on the weekends. That was just the
start of my addiction.

I went to Manhattan on Tuesdays and Thursdays. I would go
to this poetry library and write poems. It was a lot of fun and I
loved being in Manhattan. This is a place where I could live for a
long time. After writing poetry, I would go to the waterfront and
buy a coffee from Starbuck's. Then I would sit under a silver

umbrella and sip my coffee. The sun would be warm and it was really relaxing. Sometimes I would call a friend and chat for a while. Then it was a rush before the rush on the subway to get home.

We were drinking a lot and we were smoking a lot as well. Kelly and Injoon would always be with me when we drank. Most of the time it was beer, but sometimes hard alcohol, like vodka or tequila. We would talk and hang out, and then when the urge to smoke was too great, we would go outside and sit on the front steps and pull a cigarette out of the pack. Sometimes we would smoke more than one cigarette, and it was so enjoyable.

I told myself, when I was younger, that I would never smoke. My mom smoked, and my grandma smoked. Once upon a time my dad and grandpa did too, but they had quit a long time ago. I disliked the smell of cigarettes, and it actually sometimes made me nauseous. But there I was, in NYC, smoking on the front steps of where I lived, inhaling smoke and exhaling.

I never smoked when I went out. It was always confined to the house. I didn't go to too many places besides the Poet's House. I didn't go to MOMA. I didn't go to the Statue Of Liberty. I did go to Central Park once. It was really nice, but crowded with bicyclers, moms with their strollers and the quintessential tourist with their cameras flashing while eating a snowcone. So most of my time was at home.

I started to write my poems at home around the 3 week mark when I was in NYC. I ended up glued to the sofa and watching television. That was, when Kelly wasn't around. He usually crashed on the couch when he was in town. Injoon would be in his single room upstairs, and my normal place to crash was upstairs. There were 3 beds in my room, so in theory I would have 2 roommates. Most of the time, when I was sleeping upstairs, there would be only one other person in the room.

I don't remember the exact moment when I was fully addicted to cigarettes. But I was smoking more frequently since I was bored at home. I would sneak a few cigarettes in the day, then taper off in the evening. I had to be careful because a pack of cigarettes cost a lot in NYC. And my budget actually wasn't meant to spend money on cigarettes.

So I would wake up in the morning, have a cigarette, make breakfast, then plunk myself down on the couch and watch television. Then in the early evening I would write. If Kelly was in town, I would occupy the other couch, a loveseat, on the other side of the room. Frequently we would order out for food. Chinese was very popular. I would always get the orange chicken. Another favorite was Indian food. There was a takeout restaurant down the road, and I would get chicken curry with nan and white rice. I would go with Injoon when we got Indian food. Lastly, Popeye's was a lunchtime and dinnertime enjoyment. I had never had Popeye's before, and it was delicious. I always got the 6 strip meal. Injoon also accompanied me to Popeye's.

So I think now I was smoking about 5-6 cigarettes a day. The front porch was covered in ashes and the butts sticking out of the metal can that was right next to the door. When Injoon came home from English school, that's when the smoking increased. Every hour on the hour, I would knock on his door and asked if he wanted to smoke. He was always happy to, not only for the company, but because I was the one giving him the cigarettes. We would smoke and ask each other questions. He would ask me what I was working on writing wise, and I would ask him what his day was like.

So it went on like this for a while. I didn't try to stop smoking, nor did I try to curb my smoking habit. Day in and day out it was the same. We would smoke when it was sunny out, when it was raining and when it was night.

By the time my time in NYC ended, I was smoking 10 cigarettes a day. When I left on the airplane, it was going to be 5 hours without smoking. Interestingly enough, I didn't get a craving for nicotine. I flew the 5 hours without incident and made it back to San Jose.

I was in San Jose for 2 weeks. And I didn't smoke one cigarette. I really didn't think about it at all. I guess the addiction wasn't as bad as I thought it was.

The flight to Santa Fe was nice. I went there to write and to be included in the writing community there. I arrived on a Monday afternoon. My landlady picked me up in the downtown area and we became fast friends. She had a black cat, and he was really cool. I spent the first few days writing and watching television. I also read my books. My room was quite small but it was nice. The bed was comfy. I wrote on the bed, as there wasn't a desk in the room.

About 2 weeks into my stay in Santa Fe, I was walking in the downtown area. I passed a gas station. Somehow the memory of smoking came to my mind. I went into the gas station and promptly bought two packs of Marlboro reds. It was great because I could buy two packs, where in NYC I would have only been able to buy one pack. I went home, anxious to put the cigarette in my mouth and inhale the smoke.

I opened a pack and went to the backyard. I lit the cigarette and put it in my mouth. It felt wonderful and relaxing all at once. I finished the cigarette high on nicotine. I started by smoking 5 cigarettes a day, spacing out the time to smoke in 2 hour intervals. I didn't smoke after 7 pm.

After a couple weeks of this, I started to up the cigarettes smoked during the day. I was up to 10 in one day, smoking a lot when I couldn't sleep in the evenings. I remember sneaking through the quiet and dark house, trying not to wake up my roommate/landlady. I would stare at the stars and the smoke went in and out of my lungs. It was a nice diversion of getting out of the house, but I knew that the addiction to cigarettes was bad for my health.

Money was tight, and I had to start counting cigarettes to make sure I was able to smoke and buy more in the future. I would count up 5 a day. But I would still smoke 10. When the money ran out for the month, the cigarettes would too. Except for those 2 weeks at home, I was smoking every day. So when the day came when I had 3 cigarettes to smoke in 3 days' time, I felt a little panicked. The cigarettes were smoked, and I was out for the next 2 days.

I couldn't sleep well. I was going to bed and falling asleep, but then I would wake up an hour later and couldn't go back to bed. I found a temporary solution- to smoke the already smoked cigarettes. I had many, many butts, and most of them weren't smoked entirely. So I would light them up, get maybe 4-5 inhales and exhales, and then do the next butt. I made it through the next 2 days this way. Yes, I was desperate.

I went to the stop and shop in the early morning. They were still closed. I was counting the minutes until they opened so I could buy my carton of cigarettes. When they opened, I hopped into the store and bought them. I went home smoking a cigarette. It felt good smoking a real, unfinished cigarette.

I felt that just smoking was not what I wanted to do. So I started to drink again. I would wait for my landlady/roommate to leave for work, and then pilfer her stash of alcohol. At first it was a swallow. I would get high, and fall asleep in the mornings. Then another swallow in the middle of the afternoon. The alcohol almost replaced the cigarettes, but I was still getting high on the nicotine, so I would smoke right after drinking. The days were getting shorter, and I spent more time outside in the dark smoking. When my landlady/roommate came home, I would hide in my room. I would write, read and watch television. When she went to bed, I would sneak out for a smoke.

This went on for about a week. Then the effects of the alcohol were wearing off. So I started to take 2 swallows. It worked. I did this for a while, until I got sick. My stomach churned and my chest burned. I decided to stop drinking for a while. Plus, my landlady/roommate's stash was running out. She would find out for sure.

I saved up some money to buy my own alcohol. I went to the liquor store and bought a liter and a half of some really cheap vodka. I took a glass from the kitchen and filled it halfway. Then I would gulp the vodka in one swallow. I felt good. I would smoke every hour. The weather was getting colder. The sun would be out, but it wasn't warm. In a week, I would finish the bottle of vodka and the cigarettes would run out too.

An End And A New Beginning

She stood there next to the window naked. The neon lights shimmered off her body, turning her skin a purple and green. She was tired. So very tired. She put her hand behind her head and sighed. So this is it, she whispered. She put her other hand between her legs. Her clitoris was still hard.

She had been doing it for a long time. Since she was in college. It was the only way that she could pay for it. At first she liked it. Every two days she would meet them at the hotel. Same floor. Same room. Always dark. She had many. Some fat, some thin. Some handsome, some ugly. But it didn't matter to her. She liked having a dick inside her. And the money was good. Too good. After a while she would just lie there, while they would do their business. Yes, she still got wet, but it was getting boring. Plus, she worried that she would get pregnant, even though she used condoms. What if one of them broke inside me? What if the man I was with decided to rape me? She thought about these things constantly lately. So it was time.

Her son was 5 years old. His dad lived in Michigan. He was her first boyfriend. They were going to get married someday. But when she got pregnant, he fled. He fled like the coward he was, just like his dad and his grandfather before him. His dad hid in Canada as the Vietnam War raged on. His grandfather claimed conscientious objector in the world war. Once she asked him if he was sterile. He laughed and said he had never gotten a woman pregnant. They used protection. But in May of 2002, her beloved baby son was born. He didn't even stay for the delivery. When he said he would stay with her through it all, she believed him. But when the 9th month came, he was gone. Like the light after the sun went down.

She touched her breasts. They were soft and supple. She never believed in cosmetic surgery, and her breasts were quite large already. Pink nipples. She wondered how it would feel not feeling a man's hands on her. A soft snoring came from behind her. She saw an airplane fly across the star crossed sky. She went away from the window and sat at the edge of the bed. No more sex. No more slimy hands. No more lust filled eyes.

When she first had sex, it was when she was 14. It was at her best friend's house. In a closet in the basement. He was the star quarterback for her high school. It hurt. It really hurt. It hurt so much that there was blood afterward. He didn't love her. She didn't love him. It was just sex, for chrissakes. She felt empowered. She had something that could influence men. And they would be looking for it all the time.

She put her dress back on, without panties or a bra. The clouds had come and covered the moon and stars. She stood up and walked to the door. As she walked, she stepped on the sticky condom. She swiped it off her shoe and put it into the garbage can. She opened the door as quietly as possible, and shut it just as gently. She walked down the hall, and stopped at the elevator. She pressed the down button, and 5 seconds later the elevator doors opened. She walked into the elevator and she pressed the number 1. The elevator door closed and she was leaving this hotel for the very last time.

Psychiatric Ward

"I don't want to live anymore."
"We can help you."

I thought the voice over the phone said, "We can help you WITH that." I shuddered, but was still brave enough to hold the pills in the palm of my hand. The glass of warm whiskey on the table next to me. Then the voice on the line said that I should get admitted. Oh, okay. It's that easy. And I should just get up and walk 40 minutes. I could be dead in 10.

I pulled myself together and dumped the pills into the garbage can. But I took a long pull from the glass and walked into the house from the garage. My mom was sitting on the couch in the living room reading a book. I told her I needed to go to the place where I never thought I would ever set foot in. She hurriedly got her shoes on and took her purse that was on top of the piano. Nobody ever played that piano. I wondered what made me think of that.

We entered the driveway to the hospital and my mom let me off at the ER. She parked the car and I went inside. There were 3 other people there. A mother with her child. The child looked like he had a fever, as he was scarlet. I could even see the droplets of moisture on his forehead. A Latina teenager with cuts on her wrists. And an elderly man with a sling for his left arm. I sat down and my mom soon joined me. When she came, we went to the admittance window and I told them my predicament. They made me fill out some forms, and told me I would be admitted soon.

An hour went by. Then another. When the 3rd hour came, it was already midnight. And the whiskey wore off. The waiting room was empty except for me and my mom. Then a red light went on above the admittance window. A door next to the window opened, and a woman with a white smock came into the waiting room. "Steve Baba?" Yes. "Please come with me." I got up and my mom whispered in my ear that everything would be okay.

I went through the doorway and found myself in a clean, maybe too clean, room. There was a bed and a desk with a chair that had wheels on it. The nurse told me to sit on the bed and I did. She sat at the desk. A pen and paper near her. She started to ask questions. When did you start feeling this way? Did you attempt suicide before? Have you been admitted to the hospital in the last 6 months? And some questions that I didn't care to remember. I answered as best I could and then when the questions were done, the nurse said to wait. She left.

About 10 minutes later she came back in and said I was going to be admitted. We are putting you on a 5150. I weakly smiled, not knowing whether that was good or bad. An orderly came into the room and had a gurney with him. He told me to sit on it. He wheeled me out of the room and we went down a long hallway that smelled like Lysol. Then we were at a pair of double doors which had glass windows (were they glass or plastic?) and pushed a red button that was next to the doors. I heard a scratchy voice saying, "Come on in," and the doors unlocked.

We went into the place. It wasn't like anything I saw in movies or read in a book. It looked plain. There was a nurse station, and there were two nurses. One was working on some paperwork. The other was standing and waiting for us. My name is Nancy, she said. The orderly helped me off the gurney and said good luck to me. I focused on Nancy now. She said it was unfortunate that I was here, but they would try and help as much as they could. She ushered me to a room that had 2 beds and a bathroom. There were two windows with the curtains drawn. She told me that she would have to inspect me. No contraband or anything that I could use to hurt myself or others. After the once over, she said that it was late, and that I should get some rest. She turned out the light and I lay down on the bed. A little more than a cot. I drifted to sleep wondering what would happen to me. I wondered if I was a prisoner or just crazy.

Morning came quickly. The door to my room opened and it was a hospital worker. I'm here to take your blood, she said. She was young. And pretty. But that didn't matter to me at the moment. She took my arm and prepared it for the drawing of blood. It lasted all of 5 seconds. Then she left. I went back to sleep. But 10 minutes later I heard a voice echo in the room. Breakfast was to be served in 5 minutes. My stomach could use some food. I got up and dressed.

If you went down the hallway where the rooms were, there was the dining area. At least for now, I hadn't seen any of my compatriots. But when I got to the dining area, everyone was there. Only 5 patients today. They all looked the same, except their haircuts and skin color. Some had short spiky haircuts. Others long hair. Two were women. All were white except for a short, stocky Asian who had tanned skin. I felt out of place. But outwardly, I didn't see anything that showed me they were crazy.

I sat down to the table and ate a breakfast of pancakes and bacon. And some scrambled eggs. Orange juice. I was told later that I was forbidden to drink anything that had caffeine. I didn't talk to anyone. I felt alone even though there were a lot of people around me. I was missing my family. And this was just the beginning.

After breakfast I was visited by a psychiatrist. He asked a lot of questions. He prescribed me some medicine and went on his way. I was getting restless, so I took a tour of the hospital ward. There was a laundry room, a recreation room, and a meeting room.

I went into the recreation room and sat down on a couch. There was a television. I turned it on and watched Jerry Springer. After that I went back to my room for a late morning nap. Luckily I didn't have a roommate so I had the whole place to myself. A while later the intercom turned on, telling all of us that lunch was being served. I left my room and went to the dining area.

Lunch was a cold chicken sandwich with fries. A side salad, which I didn't eat, and a small carton of juice. I, for the first time, looked at the rest of the people that were here with me. There were 6 women and 2 men. Some were older. A lot older than me. There was a short, wrinkled woman with short hair that was white. There was another woman and she was a little taller, with a white pixie cut. I didn't pay attention to the others. These women were interesting to me because they were talking to themselves. I couldn't hear what they were saying, but I could see their mouths move as if some sound came out. I ate my sandwich and fries. Then I went back to my room. In there, was a man. Well he looked more like a young man. He had long brown hair and a beard. He was sleeping, so I didn't disturb him. I took a book from the ledge behind my head and read. About a half hour later, the intercom went on again. There was to be an arts and craft hour in the recreation room.

I was going to skip it, but one of the nurses came into our room, and said that we should attend. If you attend the gatherings, you may get out of here faster, she said. I got up quickly. My new roommate still slept.

I made it to the recreation room and there were three other patients there. A middle aged woman with curly blonde hair, one of the men, who was Asian with a goatee, and the short older woman who was talking to herself. She wasn't talking to herself now. A nurse was there too. She was Asian with a ring on her left ring finger. She welcomed me to the group and told me to take a seat.

There were a lot of clean popsicle sticks on the table. And some glue. There was a sheet of paper passed out to the patients. On it was a diagram of a stick figure. The nurse said that we should try to make a stick figure of ourselves. Be positive, not negative, she proposed. We each took a stick and paper that was supplied by the nurse. And some markers. I drew a picture of a smiling figure with a slim stomach and cool sneakers. Of course, I didn't have a slim stomach, nor cool sneakers. They took the shoelaces out of any shoes, so that you couldn't hurt yourself, or hurt others. I colored the hair black and a couple of red filled-in circles for the cheeks.

After a while, the nurse said that if you wanted, you could share your figures. The curly haired woman shared first. She drew a slim, straight faced figure, with a yellow sundress and sandals. She added a couple children to the figure. She explained that the children were her own, and that she hoped to be able to see them soon. The talking to herself woman was next. She showed a woman with short brown hair, a smile with teeth showing, with a pair of jeans and a t-shirt. On the t-shirt she wrote the word, "Believe." I was next, and I declined. I felt weird and out of sorts. This was not my kind of thing. Then the man with the goatee showed his figure. It was a man with a clean shaven face with long black hair and a tattoo of something I couldn't make out on his arm. The figure was wearing a tank top and shorts. The man explained that he was a hippie when he was younger, and the tattoo was genuine. He lifted the sleeve of his left arm and there was a tattoo of a carp on it. So that's what it was!

The nurse congratulated everyone, even me, and we finished. We all left the rec room and I went back to my room. My roommate was awake. I welcomed him here, and he nodded. He told me his name was Michael. I told him mine. He sat up on the bed and said he was hungry. Dinner was at 6 pm. But maybe you could ask the nurses so they could get you something before then.

That first day was not what I was expecting. I thought I was going to be visited by doctors and nurses. But the first day was just one of many that would change from day to day.

I sat next to Mike when we ate. It was spaghetti and French bread. Not that tasty, but at least it was something to eat. As usual we all ate in silence, except for the two women who still talked to themselves.

From 7 to 8 were visiting hours. My mom came and it was really good to see her. I hugged her tightly and told her that I was waiting for her all day. She smiled and handed me a clear plastic bag. In it were some books and magazines. I can imagine how boring it must be here for you, she told me. I nodded, but declined to tell her what had happened. My sisters were concerned and were praying for me. Dad was thinking about me. It was nice to hear that. I took my mom on a mini-tour of the ward. She looked with interest at each place and room I showed her. We went back to my room, and Michael was there. I introduced them, and Mom shook his hand.

When the time was up to have visitors, my mom hugged me and said she would come tomorrow. I weakly smiled as my stomach felt like there were rocks in it. I watched her go past the nurse's station, and finally through the door which held us captive.

I went to bed, but Michael was up. He was fixing his long brown hair. Soon after, he got up and I turned out the light. He came back a few minutes later and turned the light back on. I sat up and looked at him. He didn't care. I lay back down and closed my eyes. The light was on for another half hour and then Michael turned out the light.

I didn't sleep well. I was tossing and turning, and I felt hot. I tried to sleep, but I think it was because I had a roommate and wasn't sure about him. Finally, my eyes stopped looking around the darkened room and I slept.

The person who woke me up was not the nurse. It was the person who took blood and the blood pressure. I sat up as she gingerly pricked my arm. I watched the blood go into the tube. When it was full, she took it off the needle and put it into her cart. Then she took my temperature and blood pressure. She told me to have a good day and left. I went back to bed, but soon after the intercom went off announcing breakfast was going to be served. I sighed and got up.

I ate and relaxed. My anxiety wasn't as bad as it was when I first got there. But there were times when there was a punch to the stomach. They didn't come often, but I still experienced them. After breakfast was meds time. I got my pills and swallowed them down with a cup of lukewarm water.

I went back to my room. Michael was still sleeping. I started to read again. The book was really good. I looked up to see what time it was, and it was almost eleven. I continued reading and then the intercom went off to say that lunch was ready. Michael groaned and got up. He went to the bathroom and yawned. I went to the dining room and ate macaroni and cheese. It tasted really bad. But I ate it anyways. After that, the intercom came on and the arts and crafts were meeting in the rec room. I went again and saw that there were only two people in the room. One was the same nurse as before, and the other person was the short haired woman who talked to herself.

I sat down and the nurse passed out a piece of paper. On it were words that were about being positive. The nurse told us to circle the words that meant more about yourself. I circled happy, compassionate, good hearted and thinker. The nurse gave us a few moments to do it. Then the nurse said to read aloud what words we circled. The short haired woman went first. She said-She thinks about people, happy, excited and a joy to be around. The nurse put her hand on her forearm and smiled. Steve? I read my words, and it felt good to do it. The nurse clapped a few times. I was really happy. The time was up and I went back to my room. Michael was reading the newspaper. Said hello to him. He grunted back.

I wasn't sure how I was feeling at that moment. I wasn't as crazy as I was when I made that phone call to the suicide prevention center, but I still felt out of sorts. I hoped to leave the hospital though. I was getting bored and there wasn't much to do. So I made a prayer to God to make me better and that I would be able to leave.

So the next couple days were the same. I did see my psychiatrist on the 2nd day. He asked me how I felt. I told him I didn't feel suicidal, but felt off. He recommended that I stay for a few days more. When he said that I sighed really loud. He ignored it and told me to make sure to take my meds.

I just did the same thing every day for the next few days. I was getting fat. My stomach was large and it was always straining to put all the food in it. The psychiatrist told me it was because of the medicine.

Friday came, and I saw the psychiatrist again. He asked me how I felt. I felt okay. Not good, not bad. Well, he said, you can go home. I smiled and shook his hand. I started to pack and got all of my belongings into a paper bag that the nurse gave me.

I said goodbye to Michael, but he waved me off, not waved to me. He was always sleeping or reading and eating. He was just another prisoner of this place. My mom came into the hospital to pick me up. We had to get my meds from the pharmacy. The nurses waved goodbye to me and I said thank you for everything. We stepped out of the hospital. It was a clear day with no clouds. There was a slight breeze and it felt good.

A Conversation

She stood in the doorway looking shyly at the ground. "Come in!" the nun at the desk in the room told her. She walked slowly, still looking at the ground. "What do you want, my dear?" She asked if she could sit down, and the nun nodded. "Sister Anne, I had a question for you. Well, it's more like a statement." "Please tell me what's on your mind Mindy." "I want to be a nun." Sister Anne blinked twice and sat back in her chair. She knew Mindy well. An outgoing, smart teenager with a lot going for her. Sister Anne had different plans for her. She didn't think those words would have come out of Mindy's mouth. "Why?" "Because I love God. I love God so much." Mindy stared at Sister Anne. Sister Anne was taken aback by Mindy's statement. Mindy didn't do well in religious studies. Otherwise, she was the perfect student. She always was on time, never chatted while the teacher was teaching. But she didn't excel in religious studies. In fact, on one paper she wrote for an assignment, she said she didn't want to believe in God.

"Let me tell you something before you make up your mind. I know what you wrote on one of your papers to Sister Doris. You said you didn't believe in God. I can't refute the distinction of whether God exists or not."

Mindy stared wide-eyed at Sister Anne. She couldn't believe what was coming out of her mouth.

"Really?" "Yes. In fact, I was where you were a very long time ago. But ultimately I chose God. Because I had to be forgiven of my sins, and to have some spirituality in my life. If you have some time, I would like to tell you a story. It is about a young woman who traveled to Uganda a long while ago. She was there working for a church. She was a missionary. Her parents were missionaries, so she followed in their footsteps. She was 18, just out of high school. She graduated with honors. Her job for the missionary was to oversee the medical clinic. When she got on that airplane, her heart leapt. She was ready to be someone. She was ready to serve God. She wanted to do something that mattered. That would make a difference.

When the plane touched down in Uganda, her parents were waiting. They waved to her as she descended the steps of the airplane. They hugged her and told her she would do great things for God. In her mind she agreed.

She got settled in quickly. She had a room of her own and the communal showers were clean and taken care of. She wanted to look around so she put her things in her room and left the house. The first thing she encountered was dust. There was dust everywhere. The streets were dirt and nothing grew here, except the occasional palm tree. Many Ugandans were walking in the streets going somewhere or maybe going home. She liked the Ugandans. They were a simple folk just trying to survive. She remembered when there was an outbreak of cholera here a few years ago, and many people died.

She started her job at the clinic the next day. She was tired, but was very excited with her job. The first day she saw a lot of children. It seemed that there was a virus in the local drinking water and it could be cholera. Some of the children were suffering from diarrhea. She found out later that some dead animal was in the well. She felt bad for the children. They were cute and precious to her. Her first day ended with a man with a broken leg. He had fallen off a building while painting it. The doctor set the bone and put a cast on it. He would be the envy of the village, since nobody ever recovered from a broken leg.

Her first week went well. She saw a lot of different people, and most spoke some English. She talked to the doctor when there was free time, which there wasn't much of. Then came Sefi. Sefi was the local go between for the doctors and the people who couldn't speak English. He was 24, well-built and was very handsome. She took to him immediately. Sefi was an heir to a local tribal elder. He would someday be king. He was well educated, with a degree in English from UC Berkeley. She wanted to get to know him better, so she asked him if he would like to go out for a drink. He accepted and they went to a local dive bar. Some African music was blaring as they sipped their drinks. She told him she was fresh out of high school and wanted to become a doctor. Her mission in Uganda would make her resume stronger. Sefi told her about his tribe. How they were the most important one in Uganda. He told her how he had a white girlfriend in California and they were to get married once he established himself back home.

She liked him. Day after day Sefi and she would go to the bar and drink and talk. She didn't care if Sefi had a girlfriend. One Saturday, Sefi invited her to come see his family. She excitedly agreed and they went to the tribal grounds. There were small huts made of mud and straw. There were chickens pecking at the ground. There were children playing in the dust. She met Sefi's father, an older man with wrinkles where the sides of his eyes were. It seemed he liked her. He offered some water and some food. Sefi, his father and she sat in the glow of the hot afternoon sun and talked. Sefi had to translate for his father. Then Sefi took her around the grounds to see and meet the rest of the tribe. At the end of the day, she invited Sefi back to her room at the house so she could show him the pictures of her life in Massachusetts.

They sat on the bed as the kerosene light burned brightly. She showed him pictures of Boston and of her home in Wellfleet. When she felt his hand on her thigh, she didn't push it away. Soon they were kissing and then all their clothes came off. They made love through the whole night and she was so happy. Sefi twirled her long blonde hair as they lay naked in bed. Sefi told her he wasn't in love with his girlfriend anymore. Sefi wanted to tell her that he had a child from another relationship, but he held back. She slept in his arms, and as the rooster woke everyone up for the start of a new day, Sefi snuck out of the house and went back to the village.

When she and Sefi had a moment together at the clinic, they would kiss and caress each other's skin. She was falling in love and she knew it. Sefi was attentive to her and he always said the right things to her. The clinic was going well. It was getting to be the end of summer, and most people were healthy. A young man came in one day with a gash on his forehead. He said that someone attacked him with a machete. The doctor cleaned the wound and closed it. Sefi would tell her later that he was a thief. He probably got caught and was hurt from the victim.

They saw each other every day. They would see each other at the clinic during the day, then go for a beer at the local watering joint, and finally her bed. She never used protection, which was strange, since she was a very self-aware woman. She would make sure she took a shower every day, brushed her teeth and made sure she had something to eat in the morning. At the clinic she would always wash her hands after touching a patient. She was very meticulous about this. But she was reckless in bed.

After a month of seeing Sefi, she thought about bringing him back to the States and make a life with him there. She liked Uganda, but she couldn't bear to see the poverty. One morning, her stomach felt strange. She went to the toilet and threw up. Then, 10 minutes later, she threw up again. She didn't know what was wrong, so when she went to the clinic, she asked the doctor to check her out. He did a thorough examination and said that she may have eaten something bad. He told her to monitor her health, and to see him if any more sickness came. Sickness. That's what it was. Morning sickness. She was pregnant. It took her a couple days to think of it, and when she did, a cold sweat formed on her forehead. I'm pregnant? She kept on asking herself over and over, all day long. She pushed Sefi away. He was visibly hurt, but didn't know what was going on. So he left her alone. Then, when a week had passed, she told him. He smiled and was very happy. She, not so much. She and Sefi discussed options. She told him that she wanted an abortion. She knew it was against her religion, but there was nothing else she could do. She couldn't have the baby. Her parents would disown her. She would feign sickness and ask to go back to America. Sefi was non-committal. He said it was her body, so she had to make the decision on her own.

She slept badly that night. She had a dream that someone punched her stomach. She woke up in the middle of the night and the sheets were covered in blood. She knew she had lost the baby. She didn't know what to think of it. At first she blamed God, because deep down in her heart, she wanted the baby. Then she took it as a blessing, because now she wouldn't be ashamed or

have shame come to her. So she hastily cleaned herself and the
sheets up. As long as they didn't see the blood, it would be okay.

The next day she told Sefi what had happened. He laughed and
cried at the same time. She said she was going back to America.
She had already told her parents that she wanted to go home.
They didn't disagree. She put her pale hand on Sefi's black hand
and walked out the door of the clinic, never to return to Uganda.

So that's what happened, Sister Anne finished. Mindy had
tears in her eyes. Then it came to her. Was the young woman in
the story Sister Anne? Mindy wiped her face and didn't say a
thing. She turned around and walked out of the Sister's room,
never to return.

Last Request

He lay dying on the bed. He looked outside and he saw a hummingbird hover next to the window. In his weakened state even he could manage a smile. He rolled from his left side to his right side, and Abby was sitting there as always, knitting some scarf or sweater. He looked at his left arm and the tubes still were stuck in him. He sighed and reached for the table. On it was a cup of water. He was more thirsty these days. He took a sip of the lukewarm liquid and sleep started to come upon him. He lay on his back and closed his eyes.

That dream. Was it her? Was it really her? I hadn't seen her in 40 years. And there she was, standing there, whistling a tune while I was on her back. Piggyback. We did that in '93. That summer of '93. I will never forget it. She weaved through the various people on the sidewalk. It was cool. Too cool for a summer day in July. Damn, did I love her. She was the love of my life. 3 short months. Like a summer romance. But it was always summer in my heart. I wish she were here now. To see me. Yes, I am old. Yes, I'm sick. But to see her one last time. I could go to heaven then. I could let go. I could say goodbye.

He woke up. Drool was flowing from the left side of his mouth. He smelled something. It was lunch. I wonder what it is this time? He thought to himself. He sat up, and Abby was standing next to the bed. The tray was on the little table that went above his bed. She took off the cover. Beef stroganoff. It was actually hot this time. Abby took the fork and scooped a forkful of noodles with gravy on it and proffered it to his mouth. He opened and took a few chews. Wow! Just like how Mom made it.

The taste buds must still work. He ate until the plate was empty. There was an orange cut into quarters and he sucked them dry. Good, Abby thought, he still has his appetite.

There she is again. I see her sleeping on that really small bed. I think it was smaller than a twin. I can see her chest rise and fall. Her face. So peaceful. I remember kissing those glistening lips. And the lightning bolt that would hit me afterward. Then she would wake and smile at me. Good morning! I felt ashamed that I was watching her sleep. I wonder if she dreamt about me. I don't know.

He got up slowly. Abby, I need to go to the bathroom. Finally, he was able to get out of that coffin of a bed and move around. He pushed his body up. And then he turned and put his feet on the ground. Abby was standing right near him. She put her hand on his arm and lifted. He grunted as he got up. Then the shuffle to the bathroom. He deliberately went slow. Even though he could have gotten to the bathroom very quickly. He went and then shuffled back to his bed. Abby helped him settle in. He looked out at the window. A brown and yellow leaf floated by. Yes it was the autumn of his life. But then he discovered that the fire that he had in his heart so long ago was alight again. It was her wasn't it? Yes. I remember.

The letter. I had forgotten about that. I hadn't forgotten her. But that letter. THE letter. I never sent it. And then she was married. That day was the worst day of my life. I remember my cell phone ringing. Her name came on the caller I.D. I knew she wanted to tell me that today was the happiest day of her life. But I felt like crap. I took that letter and put it in a box. I saw a film once where a man whispered his secrets into a hole in a tree. Then he covered the hole with a patch of dirt. That was what my box was. That tree.

I must send that letter. THE letter. It will be the last thing I will do before I die. She needs to know. She must know. I feel inside like a 16 year old teenager, even though my body is failing. I'll tell Abby to mail that letter tomorrow.

He told her where the letter was. He told her not to ask what, where or why. She complied. He pressed the button that administered the morphine to his body. The aches were worse now. His head felt like John The Baptist's. There, all alone on a platter. He was coughing all the time. The nurses were concerned that he might catch pneumonia. They checked on him every two hours. He relinquished the fact that he could not walk to the bathroom anymore. He went in the urinal that hung on the bedside. The meals never tasted as good as that beef stroganoff. It didn't matter anyways. He wasn't hungry anymore.

Abby told him that she had sent the letter. She didn't read it. She just did what he asked for. She wondered and wondered what it was she was mailing. But being as true a spouse she was to him, she didn't ask him.

I remember. What she smelled like when she got out of the shower. That fragrant scent of lavender. I remember the fire in her eyes. It almost engulfed me entirely. I remember the softness of her body. Her breasts in my hands. I remember that room we were in. I am surprised we didn't get cabin fever in that tiny place. The drinking. I can still smell the beer on her breath before we kissed.

He rubbed his eyes. It was the 3rd night of not being able to sleep. He sat up and turned on the television with the sound off. Abby was reading a book. The show on the television was the World Cup. Spain versus England. How funny that England was playing now. That country had been on his mind for a long time now. He turned away and put his head on his pillow. He tried to sleep. His eyes closed, and he thought of that day on the beach when he cried out to her. Then the nights when the moon came out. He would make the same wish. And he wondered if she was looking at the moon too.

When he lost his ability to speak, it was exactly two weeks since he was in the hospital. At first the doctor thought that his throat was swollen shut. But it was the deterioration of the disease. He no longer had the muscle strength to speak. It was midnight when he got the call.

"Hi William. It's Bonnie. I got your letter in the mail the other day and wanted to see how you were. I heard from a friend that you weren't doing well, and I would like to see you. I live in New York now. My parents forwarded the letter to my address. Why didn't you tell me back then? I still feel the heat of your breath on my neck. I still feel your gaze upon me as I was dressing for work. Yes, I still feel that way about you. My husband passed away 3 years ago, and since the day we buried him, I wondered where you were. I hope you aren't angry at me. For being so distant all these years. For not telling you that I really felt these feelings for you. I will be on the next plane out to California. Take care, William, take care."

He couldn't eat anymore. His face looked gaunt and as if he had lived and fought in a war. His memories were scattered. He forgot that he had a wife. In his delirious state, all he could do is murmur her name, in between morphine injections. Abby was not angry at him. He talked about her all the time. Abby knew she would always be second best. But still, she loved him very much. So much, in fact, that she would be there when he left this world.

It was a beautiful day that day. She arrived that morning on a red eye from New York. She went to her hotel room and freshened up a bit. I want to look perfect for him, she told herself. When she looked in the mirror, there she was, her older self. Streaks of grey were in her auburn hair. The wrinkles on the sides of her eyes could be seen. She put on the same lipstick that she wore when she used to go out with him. She combed her hair, put on a nice outfit and headed to the hospital.

It was 10 am when she arrived. She entered the hospital and asked the info desk where he could find him. Fifth floor, room 5274. She took the elevator, and when the door opened and she stepped out, Abby was waiting for her.

"He's sleeping. He hasn't slept for a while now, so I thought if he could just sleep a little, he would be ready to see you," Abby told her.

She nodded and sat down in the lobby with Abby. She got a hot cup of coffee from the vending machine. She wondered how he would react to seeing her. She was full of questions. With no answers.

The alarm went off at 11:25 am. The nurses ran from their station and entered room 5274. Abby scurried to the room as well. A few minutes later, Abby emerged with tears in her eyes. He's gone, she whispered to her. She burst into tears. The fire in her heart engulfed her.

Hallucinations

She stood in the middle of the road. One foot each on either side of the divider. She could feel the heat of the day. It was midday and the sun was overhead. The heat came in waves, battering her lithe body. There was nobody around. The road was empty. She closed her eyes and thought of something cool. Biting into a chilled watermelon. The wind on an overcast day at the beach. A wet towel on her forehead.

Then it came. It was a Porsche 911. Black. With a whale tail. You couldn't see inside the car, as the windows were blacked out. She stood there as the car came racing at her at a frightening speed. It accelerated and it was going to hit her. Then at the last moment the car swerved to the side. She felt the air from the car. It dried the sweat on her body. The car went to the side of the road and crashed into a utility pole. She opened her eyes. There was no movement from the car. She slowly walked to it. She tried to open the door. It was jammed. She yelled. But no sound came out.

She was lying on the ground. Sweat formed on her brow and upper lip. The heat was terrific. She almost couldn't breathe. She sat up and looked around. She was on the front lawn of her neighbor. She stood up, but her legs were like oars dipping into the water. She steadied herself. The front door to the house was open. As soon as she looked in that direction, she saw a blur. Then when the blur got to her, it turned into a man. He was shorter than her. He had a crew cut and he was baring his teeth. They were as yellow as the nicotine he smoked. He opened his mouth and the most terrible sound came out. It sounded like an elephant and an air raid siren.

The sickly smell of rotten eggs came out of his mouth. She gagged and turned away. But the man followed her face. He kept on yelling at her. But she didn't hear any words. She felt faint. Her legs were buckling and her eyes closed. Then it was silent.

She opened her eyes. She felt liquid on her face. She wasn't sure if it was sweat or tears. She wiped her face with her shirt. She couldn't see anything. It was pitch black. Then she heard a noise. A dog. Somewhere near. It was barking. At what, she didn't know at first. Then she knew that the dog was barking at her. She could sense that the dog was right on her. It was circling and barking. The smell of roses was in the air. And she could taste the salt from the leftover liquid on her face. She felt something hot near her leg. It was the dog's breath. She wanted to scream, but when her mouth opened, nothing came out. Then in a split second, she felt an intense pain in her leg. The dog had bitten her.

She woke up in a room that was all white. She felt tubes near her left arm. The light in the room was muted. She sat up. She was wearing a hospital gown.

"Honey, you were dehydrated." A man in his 40's was sitting in a chair next to her bed. She shook her head. She opened and closed her eyes. Yes, she was in a hospital.

Argument

He stood in front of the lake and stared into its darkness. It was quiet and cool. Autumn had just come and the trees surrounding the lake were starting to have their leaves turn color. He thought about how the coolness in the air was like his mind- ready to do what he needed to do.

Their last argument was the worst one. She picked up a knife and told him she was going to kill herself. It was about the finances. He wasn't making enough. They would have to leave their three story house in the suburbs and rent an apartment. She was so attached to the house. The dogs were too. And she didn't work either. That made him feel angry. But he knew she couldn't work. She didn't have any skills at all. When he first met her, he saw her ample breasts and shiny beautiful face.

After their first conversation, he knew he liked her. She was amiable, cute and seemed to like to have fun. Her first drink was a margarita. He had a whiskey with soda. Then she emulated him and had a whiskey and soda. They must have drunk at least 10 between them that night. He couldn't remember what they talked about. He thought it was about sports. He never met a woman who liked sports. And baseball at that. Her favorite team was the Red Sox. His the Giants. She lamented how the new manager had destroyed the team. He agreed. When the Giants won the World Series that year, she celebrated with him by joining the countless fans in the crowd on the streets and watched the players waving.

The first month was amazing. They went out to the bars and enjoyed talking. Then it was really, really good sex afterwards.

She smoked after sex, and so did he. He would make incredible breakfasts for them- scrambled eggs, bacon, sausage, a couple pieces of buttered toast, and some hot, black coffee. Then they would wile away the morning by reading the newspaper. That is, until it got too warm in the bedroom. Then the covers would be thrown off and they would have sex again. She would take a shower and then head back home. He would dress and get ready for his part-time job at the pharmacy.

She was used to money. A lot of it. Her parents were rich, and they gave her a stipend each month to cover her expenses as well as whatever she wanted to buy. It was such an easy life for her. He, on the other hand, was used to poverty. He worked part-time jobs since his 18th birthday. His dad got him the job delivering pizzas. His dad knew the owner, and the owner knew that his dad had a son looking for work. It was fun and easy. But it didn't pay well. When he went to college, he spent all of his loan and grant money on living expenses. He rarely made it to class. But he lived decently.

When college ended, and he in a ton of debt, he found the pharmacy job. It paid well enough if he were to work full-time, but he could only find part-time work. It paid the bills. And a little more to spend after all the bills were paid off. It was also an easy job. He talked to customers, gave them their prescriptions and rang them up, and sometimes he got to type up the prescriptions themselves. But he knew he wouldn't be here for long. He had to make sure that the bills were paid, and she happy.

When they met, he was 27 and she 23. He had just gotten a new job as a construction worker. And he had the muscles to prove it. She was just moving out of her parent's house. She got an apartment not too far away from them, but far enough so she could play. And we're not talking about the games kids play.

When she moved into his apartment, she was really excited. She wanted to make over the whole place. He agreed, knowing he had no say in the matter. After she was done remodeling, the place looked like a five star hotel suite. And he was happy. And she was happy. She paid for all the remodeling herself. So he was able to keep his finances under control. They made love every day when he got home from work. It didn't matter that he was grimy and dirty from the day's work. In fact, that turned her on. He liked it too.

The air moved a little. He felt the soft breeze touch his face, touch his hair. He looked down at his feet. The water was inches away, but didn't move. He felt a soft tug on his heart. Why am I going to do this? His mind, however, was as clear as the lake. He knew what he was going to do. And it would be soon.

They got married a year later. Her parents paid for the whole thing. It was glamorous, elite and crazy all at once. At first, he didn't want a big wedding. All he wanted was his parents and brother, a best friend. She was the one who wanted big. And it was really, really big. She wanted to have all her jealous friends see her in that wonderful handmade dress by that big designer. Her makeup would be perfect. Even the shoes were custom made. He fussed and fussed, but in the end she was the one who had won out.

He didn't even remember the whole thing. The only thing he remembered was, "'til death do us part." He also remembered his brother got really drunk and hit on all the bridesmaids. He was the one who had to put his brother in a cab, and say, "Thanks for coming." The rest was a blur.

They went to Cancun for their honeymoon. She had never been there and wanted to see the clear blue skies, the clear blue water. He wasn't picky. She was always the one directing things anyways. They spent 14 days there, drinking, sunning, having scorching hot sex, and relaxing. It was good for him to go somewhere else. He had never been out of the country. She had been to many countries, by herself and with her family. He hoped they would go on more trips like this in the future.

Married life was good. He went to work in the morning, she would clean and cook. That was amazing to him, because she was so dependent. But she did her chores and errands diligently. The first couple of months went by fast. They were both entrenched in the married life. Every Saturday night they would go out to a restaurant. Somewhere expensive. Then they would go to a pub or bar. Have a few drinks. Sundays were either working on the new garden she started, or lazing about the house relaxing.

After the sixth month, things were all the same. And then he lost his job. Downsizing, they told him. But he had saved his money, and was able to stay at home. Then it got bad. She couldn't stand him being in the house all the time. She would go out to lunch every day with her friends just to get out of the house. Their first argument was who was supposed to take out the garbage. Then the fights happened almost every day. She loved him, but the sight of seeing him in his boxers all day got to her. He didn't understand. And then her parents stopped giving her her money. That sent the marriage into a tailspin.

Three nights ago, she pulled the knife out and said this was all too much. She was going to kill herself. He begged her to drop the knife. She eventually did, but not without cutting her arm with the sharp instrument. He had had enough. I'm leaving for a couple days, he said to her, not waiting for an answer.

The wind stopped and he stood there, alone as he had been for hours now. Jump in. Jump in. He could hear the words in his mind. End it. It's that simple. He took his shoes off and put his naked feet into the water. It was ice cold and he shivered for a moment. Then he walked into the water. Up to his hips, he braved the cold and decided it was time. He went waist high. Then chest high.

A pair of swans landed on the lake. They seemed at peace and they were silent. They glided on the lake surface and saw him in the water. They looked at him. At that moment, he heard a voice in his head. No. Not now. Wait. He shook his head. That wasn't what he wanted to hear. He started to go deeper. Again the voice. NO. Not now. His heart shook. Maybe this isn't the right way, he said to himself. And then he backed out and stood dripping wet on the shore.

Love At A Coffee Shop

She sat down at the table and waited for her coffee. She was tall, with blonde hair, blue eyes and smooth skin. She had a tan and was fit. She applied her lipstick to her lips, which was purple. The day was serene. A light warm wind was blowing and the sun was out. It was the first day of summer, and she wasn't going to be inside today.

It wasn't crowded at the café. There were two other tables where she was, and they were empty. Her coffee came, and she sipped it as people walked by. There was an elderly man walking his Labrador retriever. The man was bent over and had his arm extended. The leash was blue and taut. The dog was trying to make the man run. There was a woman with fashionable sunglasses on. She was walking quickly, and she seemed in a hurry. And there was a young man, no more than twenty-one. He looked at her quickly, and then sat down at one of the adjoining tables. She ignored him. She took out a book and started reading it. The young man's quick glance turned into a full on stare.

She continued to read her book. She was coming to the end, and in her mind she cursed herself for not bringing another book. The young man stopped staring. The waiter came to his table, and he ordered a cappuccino. She heard his order, and smiled. He must be a yuppie, she told herself. After that brief interruption, she concentrated on her book.

The young man was wearing a backpack. He took out a notebook and a pen. Soon he was scribbling. His cappuccino came and he took a liberal sip of it. He looked at her again, and wrote something in his notebook. Then he watched the crowds of people walk by. She looked up from her book again, and glanced at the young man. I wonder what he's writing about? she asked herself. She shrugged in her mind and read.

He looked at her intermittently, but she didn't notice. She was too into her book and sipping her coffee. He got up after a while and left. As he left, she looked up from her book and looked at him. He was quite handsome, but probably not her type. She went back to her book and coffee.

The next day was overcast. She sat indoors this time. She was wearing her glasses, as her contacts were irritating her eyes today. She found a table next to the window. She ordered a cappuccino and took out a new book, which she purchased at the bookstore yesterday. Before she started to read, she took a look around the café. There was a middle-aged couple fighting over the newspaper. They seemed to be play acting, and loving every moment of it. A teenaged girl was drawing, with a cup of hot chocolate on her table. And the usual baristas and waiters in the café.

She started to read her book and got really into it. It was a thriller, which was something she didn't usually read. It was pretty good so far. Then she looked up to look outside, and the same young man she saw yesterday was sitting in the same spot as yesterday. He looked distracted, staring out into space. He slowly took out his pen and notebook. He glanced into the café, and his eyes met hers. He tried to smile, but he felt something else. He turned away from her and started to write.

She got about a 1/3 of the way through the book, and then got tired of it. She finished her cappuccino and paid her bill. She went outside, and there was a cool wind. She tried to sneak a glance at the young man, and he was deep in thought. He was looking out into the street and sipping a latte. She went onto the sidewalk and went on her way.

It was windy this day. The sun was out, and it was lukewarm. She decided to sit outside, and maybe see the young man today. She sipped her latte and read her book. He showed up around 30 minutes later. He looked at her and he smiled. She saw him smile and smiled back. She laid back into her book and kept on reading. He took out his notebook and pen and started writing. The waiter came for his order, and he got a frappuccino. After this was served to him, he started to write in his notebook. He glanced at her every so often, adding words to his notebook. He stopped after a while and sat back in his chair, observing the nice day. The leaves on the trees were still on the trees, still green. The street was clean and there wasn't anyone walking on the sidewalk. He sighed and sipped his beverage. He noticed that she was drinking a latte, just like he did yesterday.

After an hour went by, he left. She was engrossed in her book, but something made her look up and watch the young man leave. She noticed he was wearing a pair of black jeans and a black t-shirt. He seemed well muscled. She went back to her book.

Today the rain came down, and it was wet throughout the whole city. She had her tan overcoat on, and was carrying her black umbrella. She sat inside. There was a crowd. Strange, she thought, for a weekday. She found a table near the back. She ordered a frappuccino. That was weird, because it was cold outside and a little chilly inside. She took out her book and read.

The young man came to the café 15 minutes later. He was all wet. She saw him come in and brush the raindrops from his coat. He, by stroke of luck, found a table right near her. He sat down and got a coffee, black. He took out his writing utensils, and glanced around the café. She was staring at him. She stared at him for so long, that she dropped her book. The young man picked it up and handed it to her. She touched his hand when she took her book from him, and it was hot. She noticed that the young man had deep set brown eyes, short black hair, and a goatee. She wondered how she hadn't noticed that.

She weakly smiled and went back to her chair. She kept glancing at the young man and he was deep in thought, looking over his notebook. When she looked away, he looked her way. She could feel his eyes on her, and she tried not to look. But soon, she couldn't help it, and looked his way. He was staring into her eyes. She felt herself getting warm on her cheeks. She looked away. What she didn't see was the smile on the young man's face.

He left about an hour later and the rain had stopped outside. She sighed and gathered her belongings and left as well.

Today it was really nice out. The sun was shining and the wind was slight and warm. She sat outside and waited to order her drink. She got a black coffee and sipped it, wondering when the young man would show up. She was curious about him. What he was doing, coming to the café, what he was writing and where he came from. He showed up 20 minutes later. He looked like he had just come out of the shower. Beads of sweat were on his forehead, and his hair was slick. He looked at her and waved. She waved back. He took a table a couple places down from hers. He ordered a hot chocolate and started writing in his notebook. He glanced at her every so often, and she kept her nose in her book, scared her eyes would meet his again.

As she was ready to leave for the day, a shadow covered her. She looked up and saw it was the young man.

"Hello. My name is James. What's yours?"

"My name is Dorothy. So I've seen you come here every day. What do you write about when you come here?"

He put the notebook on her table.

"Why don't you read it?"

She took the notebook and opened it. She read for about 15 minutes. Then she got up and kissed him.

Breakup

"You just don't know, Ralph."

She wiped her mouth after finishing her cigarette. Then she threw the butt out the window. Ralph, a balding man about 50 years old, fiddled with the window opener. First up, about halfway, then down all the way. All the way up, and then down halfway. All the way up, and then down all the way. The traffic was horrible; back to back car traffic for 3 miles. It hadn't been like that for a few years now, but today it was. The thick smog permeated the whole city, and Ralph was scared it would trigger his asthma.

"You are always so quiet. Too quiet. Why don't you speak? I want to know what you are thinking. Tell, me, Ralph, what are you thinking."

Ralph stayed silent. He played with the left side mirror. Left, all the way so he could see himself. The pained look on his face told himself he wasn't ready for this talk. Then all the way to the right, so he could see the scowling driver behind him. He felt like scowling himself, but he knew he wasn't capable of being angry. Just hurt.

"You know we had to talk about this sooner or later. We haven't had a talk since last month. And even then, I was the one who talked."

Ralph grimaced. Something that hadn't happened since he was a kid. He tried to smooth out the furrowed lines in his forehead, but they wouldn't go away. He opened his mouth, hoping the words would come out but they didn't.

"Ah, um," is all that came out of Ralph's mouth.

"We've been married for 22 years now, Ralph. And I don't think it's working. We aren't getting any younger. When I asked, when we were first married, if you wanted children, all you did was nod once. Nothing else. Nothing."

"Uh, yes."

Ralph finally was able to say a word. But only one word. He felt like there were nails stuck in his throat. He was unhappy. Very unhappy. She always berated him like this. But this time it felt like this argument was going to be serious. He wasn't ready for this talk, but he felt a warm sensation in his belly. Was it anger? Was it sadness?

"And, you said, when you did used to talk, that we were going to be happy for the rest of our lives. So what's happening now, Ralph? I'm not happy. Not happy one bit. Look, I have a lot of gray in my hair. It's because of you."

"B-b-b-ut darling. I love you. You know I do. I always have, and when we first met, I knew you were the one who I wanted to marry."

Ralph spilled the words out of his mouth. His tongue felt dry and he still felt those nails in his throat. But this time he was going to defend himself.

"Yeah, but you're so nonchalant. You barely speak. I see you either reading the newspaper or watching television. I can't tell whether you are alive or comatose."

Ralph felt his courage shrinking. He touch the top of his head. It was hot. A few honks came from outside of the car. Ralph thought he heard a curse word or two. He lay back in his seat and closed his eyes.

"I'm not sure how much longer I can take this, Ralph. I am thinking we need some time apart."

Ralph felt his heart drop into his stomach. He opened his eyes and stared hard at the ceiling of the car. He lifted his right arm up to grasp the wheel, and it was shaking. What he said next could mean the continuation of his marriage or the end of it.

"Dammit Fiona, I told you already that I love you. I'm always there for you. I've paid for our bills and gave you a nice house to live in. What more do you want?"

"You're a liar. You don't love me. All you do is say things you don't mean. That's why you don't say anything. All those lies coming out of your mouth."

Ralph felt defeated. She always won the arguments. There was no way to convince her what he was saying was true. He slumped in his seat and waited for the car in front of him to inch forward.

It was quiet in the car for quite some time. They didn't look at each other. Fiona had her arms folded on her chest. She wanted to argue even more, but knew it would be futile.

Ralph fingered his wedding band. He wanted to take it off and throw it out of the window. He had had enough of her insults. He took off the band and put it in his hand.

"Here. Take it. You've taken everything else. So you might as well have this too."

Ralph dropped the ring into Fiona's hand. She looked at it for just one second. Then she rolled down her window and dropped it. It bounced a few times on the pavement. Then it rolled under a car.

Revenge

The small boy sat on the seat with a sling on his left arm. He had a headache. His mom was sitting next to him reading a magazine. The doctor was to come soon. Apparently he fell down a flight of stairs, injuring his arm and sustaining a concussion. It was an accident, his stepfather told his mom. But the boy knew better.

When the doctor came, he smiled at both the boy and his mom, and ushered them into the examining room.

"How are you feeling?" the doctor asked the boy.

"My arm aches and I have a headache," the boy replied.

"Let's take a look at that arm."

The doctor gingerly took the arm out of the sling. He looked it over, and then started to move it slowly. He asked if this hurt, if that hurt. The boy nodded without a look of pain on his face. The doctor told his mom that the arm would have to be in a sling for a couple days. Then the doctor prescribed some painkillers. For the head and the arm. The boy and his mom left for the pharmacy.

"Mom, I want to tell you something, but I don't think you'd believe me."

"Go ahead."

"Nah. It's okay."

"Are you sure?"

"Yeah."

They got the painkillers and went home. As their car pulled up to the driveway, the front door opened, and a handsome, tall man stood at the doorway. On his face was a genuine look of concern. Bobby felt sick. But the wave of nausea went away, and he followed his mom into the house.

Mom cooked a special dinner that night. She made spaghetti and meatballs with a nice red sauce. She made garlic bread and didn't even make vegetables. Bobby ate as if he were starving. He really enjoyed his mom making his favorite meal. Joe ate in silence, while Bobby and his mom discussed what they were going to do this summer. Bobby had only a week left, and his mom suggested that, when his arm and head felt better, they go to the beach. She knew he liked making sandcastles and swimming in the nice cool water. Long Island was a perfect place for a child to enjoy his summers. Bobby, on the other hand, felt scared. Mom worked during the day. Joe worked from home. Bobby would be alone with Joe. This did not sit well with Bobby.

Bobby went to bed. His mom gave him the painkillers, and then read him a story. She kissed him on the forehead, turned on the nightlight, and turned out the lights. She told him to sleep with the angels. Bobby slept well that night. His arm hurt less, and his headache was gone. When he woke up in the morning, he got up, used the bathroom, and went downstairs. Joe was waiting for him at the dining room table. There was a couple of poached eggs with some bacon and a couple pieces of toast on a plate for

Bobby. He ate his breakfast in silence and didn't look at Joe at all.

"So it was good of you to not say anything, Bobby."

Bobby kept his head down.

"Remember, it was an accident, nothing more, nothing less."

Bobby could feel tears starting to form in his eyes. He cleared his plate and went into the living room. He knew what Joe was trying to tell him. If you tell, it will get worse, is what he was saying. Bobby watched cartoons on the television until he had to go to school. He went back upstairs, dressed for school, and went back downstairs. He opened the door and closed it gently. He knew Joe didn't like loud noises.

Bobby's teacher was concerned. She knew that in the preceding months that Bobby had various hurts on his body. Some were visible, some weren't. But Bobby never complained or seemed different, so she didn't make anything of it.

Today was the day where the teacher was going to teach how to write. She told the students to take out a piece of paper and a pen or pencil. Just write what's on your mind. Don't worry about content or grammar. Just write. Bobby had nothing to write about. In fact, he had a lot on his mind and wanted to write, but didn't. He eventually wrote about aliens. Bobby liked aliens. He watched a lot of movies where there were aliens. His favorite movie was Independence Day. After he was done, he turned in his paper. Then the bell rang and it was recess time.

"My dad yells at me when I've been bad," said George. George was Bobby's best friend.

"He does it a lot because I'm always getting into trouble, but he's never hit me or anything like that." Bobby didn't mention anything pertaining to Joe.

"So what happened to you?" Bobby told George that he slipped on the stairs and fell. It was an accident.

"Well, if I were you, I'd be more careful. You could have broken your neck or something really bad." It won't happen again, Bobby thought to himself.

Recess was over and the rest of the day went fine. Lunch was good. Bobby and George ate together. Bobby had a hot lunch made at the school and George brought his lunch from home. George always let Bobby have his cookies. They got through afternoon class, and then all the kids were let out for the day. When the final bell rang, Bobby felt his stomach churn. Not again. Not with him. I can't go on this way. I want to die. Bobby opened the door and ran upstairs. He hoped he wouldn't see Joe. Joe wasn't around. Bobby went to his room and shut the door. He wished he had a lock on his door, but his mom forbade it. Bobby went to his desk and started to draw a picture with crayons. He drew a face that was green, black and red. He put lightning bolts on the head for hair. Bobby heard the front door close. It was him.

Bobby stayed in his room until 5 pm. That's when his mom came home. Joe was in the study doing his computer graphics work, and wouldn't have his mind on the boy today. Plus, he thought to himself, he needed to heal.

Bobby's mom came home early. She wanted to make sure Bobby was alright. She went into his room and Bobby was reading a book.

"How's my little darling?"

"I'm fine, Mom. My arm is still a little achy, but I haven't felt anything in my head for a while now."

Bobby's mom hugged him, and she put her hand under his chin. She looked at him for some time, and then told Bobby that she was going to make dinner.

This time, it was Joe's turn to not look at Bobby. There was a heaviness in his heart, and he felt bad. Poor kid, he thought. He's only 8 years old. He regretted the past and told himself he would stop drinking. It was affecting his work. Joe ate in silence, while Bobby and his mom chatted about school. He told her about the starting of writing in his class. Bobby's mom was excited for him. He told her about his story about the aliens, and she laughed. You sure like aliens, Bobby's mom said. Bobby smiled and finished his dinner. Then Bobby went to the living room and put in a movie to watch. It was Independence Day.

When the movie finished, Bobby could hear loud voices coming from upstairs. It went on for a while, and then died out. Bobby's mom stormed down the stairs. Joe came to the top of the stairs and yelled.

"Barbara! Come back here!"

Barbara went to Bobby's side and sat next to him. She stroked Bobby's hair and told him he was a good boy. I know, Bobby, I know. We'll do something about it. He is an awful man. Bobby cheered up. He's gone!

The next day was a good day for Bobby. He was able to take the sling off and went to school very excited. He wrote a story about a fish that swam from a river all the way to the ocean. It was a cheery, very well described story. His teacher was impressed. Bobby played with George on the playground. Then the call came. Bobby was to be excused and picked up by Joe. Something had happened. Bobby's mom was in a car accident.

Joe picked up Bobby in front of the school. Joe was quiet. Bobby felt a little dizzy. They went to the hospital. Bobby's mom had died. Bobby started to cry. His mom was the best thing in this world. A couple days later they had the funeral. Bobby's heart hurt. And he was getting scared. All alone with Joe now. Now what would he do?

Bobby was alone on Saturday afternoon. He went to the kitchen and took a knife out of the drawer. He drew a line on his wrists with the knife. How could he do this? Why was he doing it? He almost had no choice. Better to be with his mom in heaven than be with that monster. He put the knife back into the drawer and started to cry.

Joe was drinking that night. His poison of choice was vodka. When he drank he got angrier and angrier. When Joe was like this, Bobby stayed in his room. But tonight Joe would come into Bobby's room.

The door slammed open as Joe stood in the doorway. Bobby got up from his desk and stood in front of him.

"Go ahead and do it, Joe. You know you want to."

Joe's face turned crimson with anger. He took his arm and swung it. The splash of pain throbbed in Bobby's left cheek. Joe turned Bobby around and took his arm and pulled it behind Bobby's back.

"You little shit. You are nothing. All you do is sit around, eat, and take up space."

Joe pulled Bobby's arm even higher, and Bobby cried out. After a few seconds he let go and Bobby slumped to the ground.

"Remember, small fry. I am the master now. Your mom is no longer here."

Joe slammed the door shut and tears formed in Bobby's eyes. He felt his heart drop to his stomach. Mom, oh Mom, where are you now? He thought.

Bobby had a strange dream that night. He dreamt that his mother was still alive. She took him away to the beach. He went into the water and swam out into the open ocean. When he turned around and tried to swim back to shore, there were large stones in place of his arms and legs. He started to drown and then he woke up. Bobby got up and looked out the window. There was no moon or stars to see. Bobby went back to bed and thought. He was wondering what he could do to Joe to make him stop. He could tell the police, but they wouldn't believe him because Joe was an ex-cop. He could tell his teacher, but all she could to is report it to child protective services, and Bobby knew full well how reliable they were. So he felt so low that he didn't know what to do. But he remembered that writing was something that he could escape to, so he went to sleep and thought about the future.

The first story Bobby wrote was about Joe. He was with Joe at a swimming pool. Joe was at the edge of the pool and Bobby was right next to him. Bobby pushed Joe into the pool and Joe splashed into the water. Joe didn't know how to swim. He floundered and floundered until he sank to the bottom. A few minutes later Joe's body bobbed up and down, face down, on the water. Bobby thrust his arm into the air and then pulled it down violently. YES! He said. Joe was dead.

The second story was just as shocking. Joe was at the top of the stairs, and Bobby right behind him. As Joe descended the stairs, Bobby pushed him. Joe fell to his death in 10 seconds. There was a pool of blood next to Joe's fractured skull. Bobby smirked and said to himself, that's what you get you abuser. You pushed me down, now I push you down.

When Bobby finished writing the 2nd story, he felt good. He really enjoyed writing these stories. They were tame in comparison to Stephen King, but they were shocking nonetheless. Bobby continued to write these morbid stories, each getting worse and worse.

A week or so later, Joe ended up drunk in the afternoon. It was a Saturday, and Bobby was in his room. George was out of town. Joe went to Bobby's room and slammed the door open, just like before. He pulled Bobby from his chair and shook him violently. Then he slapped Bobby on both cheeks. Finally he punched Bobby with his fists on Bobby's back. He left. Bobby was not hurt, but angry. He vowed to get back at Joe in his stories.

Bobby wrote a story where a man came into the house, found Joe in his study. The man had a knife. He plunged it into Joe's back and then left. Joe bled to death and without any help. Yes, Bobby said to himself, that's the way I want him to die.

Saturday night. Joe was drunk again, but left Bobby alone. Bobby was curious as to what Joe was doing. He quietly walked down the stairs and peered into the study. Joe was looking at pornography. Bobby felt uneasy. Then he heard a noise. He stood right next to the door and was silent. He saw a shadow. The shadow crept into the study. Then a glint of steel. A flash, and a knife was plunged into Joe's back. Blood spurted out. Bobby felt hope in his heart. Joe fell to the ground and started to whimper. Then his body went stiff. He was dead. Bobby felt relieved. He's gone, finally gone, Bobby whispered. He thanked the shadow and called 911.

Vignettes

I

Are you in love? Are you? Well? I'll tell you soon. It's been a long time. She reached in and pulled out the dagger in my heart. Today is the first time I laughed when it rained. Don't change. Don't change. My goodness, this chocolate bar is delicious! And it would taste sweeter if you shared it with me. Take off your glasses so I can see your eyes better. Let the rose wind go into your hair. Maybe we'll get a glance of butterflies. There are some in my stomach right now. I like your smile. Is that okay? I feel the life pulse of love coursing through my veins. What a coup.

II

They called me crazy. That you wouldn't get anything happy. But then you were there. Just there next to the daisies. Tingles in my arms. Hair lightly toasted. Where was your face before I knew you? This song is not meant for dancing. You are smart. You are wonderful. No mistakes this time. And I will not think about winning or losing. Frozen. Then thawed out. Hell, there might still be life in this old body of mine.

III

Sweet. And also mountains with snow beauty. There was a time when loneliness was welcome. The tea is getting cold. Time to take you in my arms and say something that I will regret. Or maybe not. No locks. No chains. And you said you didn't cry. Liar! Liar! Pants on fire. Just like your hair. Did you read that story in the newspaper? 65 years. Wow. And then I thought about how we would look with our still matching gold rings and only the keys that had been chasing us for so long. Beauty. How your eyes still burn dynamite.

IV

She fell in love like she scratched an itch. Where are the ice cubes? She took the ring he gave her and put it in her palm. Just like holding his heart. Diamond eyes, will you seek me out? Forever. Forever. Forever. And it should be that way. Grow old. Grow old together. Let the groove of your body make us a complete puzzle. Martini. Dirty martini. Vodka martini. Gin martini. They are all different. Just like the ways she loves him. Get me a glass of water please. I will stay as long as the tea holds out. Or maybe I'll stay a little longer.

V

Get on your knees and remember that it was a dark day when the cross was a shadow on the hill. Apples and oranges. Water and oil. Sand and sea. That's us. You knew that. Very strong wind today. The newspaper said that if you run away from life, you are as good as dead. Help. Help me. Help yourself. Take the broom and sweep the shards of solitude and quiet into the morning portal.

VI

One last thing. Take this hand and hold it for as long as you can. Then let it go. It was easy to look at something as beautiful as you. Kisses come in spurts. Hugs rare these days. Break the sapphires. Put perfume on your happiness. But really, really don't do what I will tell you now. Never let the moon take away your hope. She will only throw it over the horizon and let her lover the sun destroy it.

VII

A thousand apologies. A thousand I love you's. And they say that happiness is dead. Go. Go. Go. Run to the light and never turn back. All my life a diamond ring was not in my budget. So I gave you a ring from the Cracker Jack. Gather your smiles and put it in this plastic container. I will shield my eyes. I will use them when I am lonely or sad or hopeless. A locket of auburn hair. Cream colored skin. And I have not seen anyone who could knock me off the stool and drink my beer all at once. Truth is good. Trust is better.

VIII

Does barbwire wrap around your mind? Took the memory train to 16th and Mission. I dropped off my worries into the garbage can. Down the river there was this old man. He taught me how to swim. He taught me that women were sacred. I believed him. And he was right. Teeth show when the lukewarm light opens the deep chasm of tongue and throat.

IX

What is that locket around your neck for? What is that ring on
your finger for? Love you silly. I am silly? Of course you are.
Now go get some ice cream and listen to Miles Davis. The
cigarette can wait. The stars can wait. But don't make me wait
with my hands and arms up in the air. How else will I be able to
hold the one thing that means the most to me? Drop. Pick up.
Scoop. Shuffle. I can see my reflection when I look at your face.
The emeralds fall to the ground. What does it mean? Take your
hat off.

X

The double is not enough to make me dizzy. The 5 from 10 is less than the change that I carry in my pocket. Oh I see now. Leaving me wasn't enough. You had to take my favorite shirt. You never washed it. What does that mean? I am yours forever. I am like melting ice cream. Still sweet even if my body doesn't hold up. Maybe that's what happens when you turn 80.

XI

Do you know what love is? Do you? Do you? She lay next to me sucking the dripping love from her fingers. Something so beautiful touched my eyes. Vegetables. Noodles. Meat. Chinese never tasted so good. Did you bring your compassion to me? I saw it come through the door and kiss my cheek. Baby can't you see- you're the only one. My high is your high. Snow falls on the mountain. This is the place where only we can exist.

XII

I'm intrigued. She hides behind those black framed glasses when I can see a woman who is confident and happy. I look at her mouth and wonder what it would be to kiss it. The temperature gets higher and higher. I'm softening like a melting ice cream cone. Her hair falls in front of that Matisse painting of a face. Picasso would be envious. Even his Russian dancer bride was not as pretty. All I think about is feeding her slices of apple dipped in peanut butter. When the time comes I will slip that gold ring on her finger. I saw this a long time ago. I see it now. I will see it in the future.

XIII

Behind me I hear her walking. Trying to catch up. Trying to look into my eyes. There is no blackness in them. Only the bright yellow and green that caught her breath when we first met. She holds a book in her hand. She so desperately wants to recite Neruda. That guy knew what he was talking about. Love. Love. Love. I am the ocean to her sailboat. I am the brow on which she perspires. I am the lips that are painted by her slender fingers. Someday I'll realize that she was the one. And I can be selfish. And I can be self-centered. But her sugar will sweeten my bitterest frown.

XIV

I see your point. But why does it matter? I know when my heart speaks it is talking to hers. Almond eyes. Raven black hair. Smooth creamy skin. She's read more books than a librarian. She asks the right questions. She deciphers the right answers. I was the one that she couldn't figure out. The only puzzle she couldn't put together. A perfect day. Ripe green apples. So sour. But so good. I lay my head in her lap and stare up in the sky. Yes, we are seeing the same sun. Yes, we see the same clouds. Are they waiting for something? Kiss her? Kiss her.

XV

You believe in the love that carried you from birth to death. But what about her love? She was the only person who could make you squeeze your eyes shut and a wish would come true. Can't you understand? There is no malice. There is no bitterness. Only the roses that dance under your nose. How I wish you could listen to the birds sing and play in the water at the bottom of the road. Half worried, half sad, and maybe a little anxiety thrown in for good measure. But her. The calm wind. The slice of cold watermelon on a hot day. Wish for her. Wish for her.

XVI

A day like today. When the breeze is sweet. When the tongue
tastes the light of the sun. Now she's flying. Now she's floating
above the clouds. Look at her dance! A swan in a mirror still lake.
A butterfly on the wind. The hummingbird taking in the nectar of
the flowers. How did I miss you? The first fly by was quick. I
only saw your fingers and toes. The second I got to catch a
glimpse of a perfect sculpture. And finally there was your heart
singing praises to mine. Don't forget that when you rest, think of
the sighing clouds when they touch the sky with their beautiful
shapes and sizes.

XVII

I thought I saw you hiding behind a cloud. Were you peeking at me? I wish I could see your eyes better. What was that? You miss me? I like the way you smile. That's when I can see you smile. Lovely day. I could go out for ice cream and a bottle of ice cold water. I'm drifting towards you. Am I falling too? What if I could say everything that lay in my heart? Would you take all of it and lock it into yours? I want to live a life free of sadness. Wash my sins away. Take a look at the mirror. And see how beautiful you are. Yes, you are.

XVIII

Someday I'll be next to you. I can feel your heat. You can feel mine. Look at the setting sun. It reminds me of you. This world keeps on turning. This candle is burning in my heart. Life is strange. Just when you think you figured it all out you get whacked on the back of your head. You get a twist somewhere inside and hope that this feeling lasts long. Or at least for a while. Carry us away you naughty wind. Take us where we can enjoy the taste of the last strawberries on earth. The daisies are on the table. They are sad because they want to be in a vase full of water. Somehow we are here today. The dream is still alive.

XIX

Touch my lips with your fingers. They tremble. They curve into a smile. Red is not my favorite color. Blue is. Just like the ocean. Where are you, ocean? Swimming in my mind. Hovering above me in the sky. Oh, that's the color blue again. Deep breathes. Keep your brown eyes open. You can look at me if you want. It's okay. What do you see? You tell me you see someone who is good. A good person. It is nice to hear that from you. You are lovely too. Make sure you keep the good thoughts in your head. Be well. Be well.

XX

Every time I lose my way, the light of your soul finds me and puts me right again. I like it when the lake mirrors the cascades. I like it when the mountains speak to me about beauty. Your beauty. I am a lucky man. You always took care of me. You always held me when I was cold. You always smiled when my heart was down. There is only a lightness in my step. I see you are skipping. I wish I could be like that.

XXI

Was I crazy for you? Or was I just crazy? The trees are swaying in the wind. The dandelion seeds fly into the air. How I wish I were with you right now. I want to hold you in my arms and smile at you. What song would it be? Probably some sappy romantic song. But how the notes would be clear. How the voice would be resonating. The dream of grey dolphins swimming above me as I breathe in the cold blue water. After all this time I would hope you would know me. How the moon blinks into your brown eyes. How the stars see what I cannot see. Your inner beauty. Your happy countenance. There are no regrets. Only a will to love.

XXII

Drink the nectar of the Gods. Get drunk on life. Get drunk on love. I'm enjoying the day. Soft pillow. Soft blankets. We will have a fun time holding each other. We will be like two peas in a pod. I left my bitterness at the door last night. I have beaten the sorrow. I have conquered the despair. Now all I have left is you. Strike my anvil heart with your gorgeous hammer. The temperature is hot and getting hotter. You are a living ghost of delicious food. You are the good person I always wanted to be.

XXIII

These feelings. So confusing. I don't know what to do. I see you sitting near me. I'm sipping my coffee. You are eating a peach. I see you look at me. Then down. Then at me again. What are you thinking? The sparkle in your eye makes me swoon. We were meant to be together. Touch your lips with your delicate fingers. Blink with wonder. I can't wait until I leave for work. I can't wait for that goodbye kiss. Rest assured, I will always be there for you. Always there for you.

XXIV

You are the burning in my cheeks. You are the sugar on my
tongue. The breeze is sweet. The grass growing quietly on the
ground. I found a pebble in my shoe. It reminded me of you. The
ripples in the lake distort the reflection of the mountains. All is
snow. All is bright. I caught a glimpse of you in the morning.
How beautiful. How beautiful. I will always take away the good.
Leave behind the bad. Follow my path and we will be happy. We
will be happy.

XXV

I rub my eyes. I can't believe what I'm seeing. That porcelain face.
Those penetrating brown eyes. Where is the justice? I am always
forgetting the times when we would not be around each other. I
guess that that is alright. A robin pecks at the dirt around my feet.
The heat on my neck almost unbearable. I sought your cool water.
You cleansed me of my bad thoughts. You blessed me with
goodness. And then the kite in the sky danced on the wind. And
then the eagle soared high in the skies.

XXVI

When I told you I loved you, it was meant to be a message from my heart to yours. My head spins. My body wants to dance. I'm ecstatic. I'm so high I can't see the ground beneath me. The cigarette burns between my fingers. I can't catch the smoke. But somewhere, somehow, I will be with you. The ice breaks. I take the ice cold water and get a drink. The coals in my heart still burning. You will show me the way. I will show you the way. Back to our happy childhoods. Back when we cared only for the sun and moon.

XXVII

Why did I just think of you this moment? I miss you I think. I heard your laugh in my ears. That was fun. That was the breaking point. Someday you will tell me that it will be okay. My beard grows longer. The shadows in my eyes grow longer. But the smile on my face is genuine. The twinkle is still there. I found my way to you when I needed you the most. Dimples swimming in cinnamon. There is only a joy that only you can understand. There are no faults here. I feel good today. Let the daisies follow the wind and into your nose. Let the expression of gratitude be your sword. Let the hard shell of loneliness break until you can see light. You can see light. I know I can.

XXVIII

There will come a day when I step out of the shower and you will suddenly kiss me. The dripping water falling on your lips. A glass of orange juice. A bowl of cherries. Those cherries. Always sweet. Always sour. We weren't perfect. But we tried. And it worked. My hands are going to hold yours. My face will be in a soft light where you can see how happy I am to be with you. I will never fake happiness. I will always think of you when I am waking up. When I am working. When I'm on my way home. It was never impossible. It was never wrong. And the sun will shine. And the warmth will keep us together. Just don't forget the moon and stars. They are our friends too. They are also lovers.

XXIX

When I'm next to you, what do you feel? The candle burns so
brightly. That love song on our beat up radio. The cool water still
delicious. The worry on my face disappears when you touch my
cheek. My breath so calm. My arms so relaxed. Bring me a bagel
with cream cheese. We can share it. I'll bring a dash of goodness.
You bring the flame of hope. All is beautiful. All is satisfied. All
is mellow. All is kisses and hugs. In the morning. In the
afternoon. In the night. It's always Sunday afternoon in my mind.

XXX

There is a tiger in my heart. It wants to roar. It wants to love. It wants to scratch away the film of sadness from your face. I remember when you used to walk on the sidewalk and get the men to watch you all the way to the subway station. I remember when you used to whistle our song while taking a shower. Nothing breaks me. Nothing perturbs me. We'll always have San Francisco. We'll always have the cool wind blowing into our hair. I'm still alive. You are too. And that is the most important thing.

XXXI

Daydreaming when I will see you again. I can see you so clearly.
Like a mountain with snow on the peaks. Like the river that flows
so easily through the canyon. Like the pencil that writes that first
good word on paper. The golden sunshine is delicious. I want to
eat an apple. My worries go away when I feel the wind on my
back. How I wish I could send my love in an envelope and give it
to you. And then I know it would make you happy. The darkness
hid her beauty but I still saw it. The black hair falling on her
shadowed face. A glint from her eye. When the light came it was
not disappointing. Nicotine high. Falling stars. God only knows
that the laughter would be bold. A broken apple. A sad face on
the orange. Please forgive me for being too happy. My face was
perfect. My life not complete until the owner of my heart,
contemplating the series of events, that would make me love her.
Forget the glow. Remember the funny. Remember the interesting.
Remember the coolness of breath on my shoulders and neck.

XXXII

Grip the towel. Let it absorb the moisture. And then being dry wasn't so bad. A shower with good tidings. I believe in it now. Could it be that the cleansing be a motive for happiness? I think so. I think so. Grip the soap in your hand. Wash the shampoo away. I like it when the sun shines through the window and the birds are singing. The glow after brushing your teeth is hot. Very hot. Keep the water running. Keep the life going. That is all that is left now.

XXXIII

He sleeps. I see his eyes move. I wonder what dream he is having.
Maybe of her when she was still beautiful. No makeup. No
lipstick. Just natural beauty. And she tossed her hair back into the
light. When the light went down beyond the horizon, her eyes
sparkled. Like the stars that were soon to come. The moon
brought her face closer to perfection. And he smiled. For a long
while. For an infinite amount of time. Who wouldn't be happy
with a woman that looked like the forest. All green and nurturing.
Like a flower that had just bloomed in the middle of a silent
pasture.

XXXIV

She was endangered. Like an animal. But more graceful. Scratch that itch before it runs away. Catch her soul before she runs away. Be good. Be good. And please hold on to the word that means most to me. Sitting on a chair. Reading a book. I like to see that tear fall from your vivid blue eye and tell me that everything is good. Everything will be okay. Good to know that you are still passionate and compassionate. Good to know that you bring the breeze with you and make life easier for me. Whether it is good or bad I don't care. I want to tell you too that my heart soars when I hear you sing. Hear you sing. Take the blanket and keep yourself warm. Take the peach and enjoy its juices. There are no bad feelings. Only good. Only good.

XXXV

I forgot your name one time. It was just an honest mistake. But I remember your heart. Still jumping like an antelope in the tawny grass. I saw you when you were at your worst. But even butterflies envied your beauty. A moon so bright I thought it was the sun. The stars still absorbing the love you kept so secretly. The laughter died, but I still heard the music. The life of my sadness coming to its expiration date. I want to have the lovely robins say your name. Say what you couldn't say. When your eyes smile it makes me want to jump off a cliff and open the parachute right before I hit the ground. Yes, impact is vital. To make the stray tears collect in an old glass bottle.

XXXVI

This coffee tastes bitter. Where is the sugar? Where is the cream? The barista is cute. Too cute. She walks around listening to orders and filling cups. I think I want to tell her she is cute. I would probably follow her around like a puppy dog. Maybe she hid the sugar so I have to listen to her sweet voice. There is a nice small rose in a cup of water on the counter. Maybe I should steal it and give it to her. He laughs out loud and says words that don't make sense. Maybe he had too much coffee.

XXXVII

That tingle down my spine. I wish she were here right now. I could tell her news. Good news. The world has stopped. And now I have the time to tell her how I feel. I'd tell her I'd show her the way. Let the whispers come and go on the wind. The sound of my heart still following her. When I think of her it's golden. I have drifted almost too far away. But I'm here now. And it has been one road with too many rocks and dirt on it. Let me sweep her off her feet once again. Once again.

XXXVIII

A sunset. This is where love begins. Caught something in my eye. It was a diamond. It is for you. Free at last, to be myself. To be the person you always wanted. Someday we'll look at this time and realize that it has been a great many happy thoughts. What am I doing wrong? Nothing? That's good. Bring me your eyes and mesmerize me once again so I can remember what joy is. Was. Will be.

XXXIX

Coffee still coming and going down the throat. It's filled with cream and sugar and love if then that would be way too easy to live tomorrow and today and funny and laughing and crying and praising and jumping and catching the cold of our resistant century this was a good idea to tape the dollars to your arm and flexing the sturdy sun onto the clouds that seem to be the hidden secrets of an imaginary daffodil saturating drinking and lifting to the highest mountain of art in the foolish veins that poke through my sides my feet my head. Go please. The woman is waiting with her golden smile. The woman is sitting with a golden heart.

XL

How I wish you were here to enjoy the good times and make it through the bad times. You mind is filled with sugar balloons and your heart a piece of steel against the anvil. Remember that cafe we used to go to? You with your rain drenched red hair, a glistening tear of dew falling from your eye. Was that really a tear? I don't think so. I bought the coffee, and brought it to our table. You realized that you never had to add honey or milk or sugar to it. I knew just what you wanted. I thought your eyes were looking through me. They probably were. What did you see? A fool who loved the most compassionate of women? Or the goof who played Dungeons & Dragons on the weekend? Ah, but see this too- an arrow. A bow. A small child shooting the arrow into my chest. I was never ready for that. Or anything for that matter.

Merced Diary

Hi. My name is Steve and I will be your companion for the next few pages. I'll be talking about a lot of different things. So let's get started, shall we?

I live in Merced, California. I saw an article listing the 10 most dangerous cities to live in in California. Guess what? Merced was on that list.

I've been here for 6 months. I actually lived here in 2013 for about 6 months. I have gotten used to the scorching hot summers and rainy winters. I like this city, and even for a small town there are things to do.

I have a few good friends that are artists, musicians, writers, poets and actors. The further I go into this discussion, the more I'll talk more about my friends.

There are cockroaches. Many, many of them in the summer. When I go outside to smoke in the evenings, I see them scurrying on the cement by the garage. I am used to them, as when I would go to Hawaii, they had them there. And huge suckers, that flew. My roommate hates them, and she squishes as many as she can when she is with me smoking.

The summers here are hot, hot, hot. In the upper 90's or low 100's throughout the summer, and into the fall. I always get tan when summer comes around. It's best to stay indoors when it gets that hot. Thank goodness we have air conditioning.

Wintertime this time around was very mild. It reminded me of San Jose, where I was born and bred. But for some reason we paid a lot of money on heating. I'm not sure if we got ripped off from the electricity company, but it sure feels like it.

I have not lived here in the spring. I'm sure it will be lovely. It'd be nice to see the flowers blooming, the trees blossoming. Before I lived here for the 2nd time, I lived in San Francisco. SF does not have seasons. It's either cold, or colder.

I have this aloe vera plant that my neighbor gave me. It's a really nice plant. It's small, but should grow. I like succulents and aloe is one of my favorite plants.

I'm going to finish here until tomorrow. Tomorrow's subject, a little more about myself and a little more about the city of Merced.

So, first of all, I'm 43 years old. My birthday is coming up next week, and I'll be almost, if already, middle-aged. I really feel like a teenager, and think like a man in his twenties. I still have wants and dreams that I want to happen, and that makes me feel good. I'm Japanese-American. Fourth generation. I was raised in an Asian environment, but my life as an Asian started and stopped when I came home from school and when I left for school. Even my friends were not Asian. I was brought up at a time when our great country was progressive, and that the hate and violence that has happened these last few daunting years would have never happened. My parents were strict but loving. I have two sisters. Both younger than me. They both have kids. I'm single and have been for quite some time now. I've never been married.

I've been a writer for a long time. When I was in elementary school, I wrote two fantasy novels. I used to have them stored away in a storage unit, but unfortunately I don't have them anymore. I started writing poems after I got out of high school. But the prose has been with me since I was little, and continues to this day. I have two best friends. My first, Lance, I have known since elementary school, and he is also a writer. We wrote together in class when we had free time. Jim, my second best friend, is younger and thinner than me. He is a merchandizer at a San Francisco music venue. Lance is a physics high school teacher. Lance still writes, like me.

I am easy going and am kind and generous to most people. And to those I am not, I don't step on their toes. I have never hated anything (well, perhaps certain vegetables) or anyone in my life. I drink a lot of water and hot chocolate. I listen to a lot of music. And I am fond of the books that J.R.R. Tolkien wrote.

So that's me in a nutshell. Tomorrow I shall introduce to you my friends in Merced. They are an eclectic and awesome bunch of friends.

Ben is a musician/artist/poet. He's a nice guy with long dirty blonde hair and a few days growth beard. He wears glasses. He is a Ph.D. candidate with the local college here. He's mellow, likes to smoke pot and is brilliant. I met him the first night I went to the local poetry open mic. We usually get together on Tuesday afternoons to write poetry. He also is the publisher of TREE, a poetry magazine based here in Merced. I think he is a great artist and I cherish the times when we get together.

Melissa is the owner of a coffee shop, called Coffee Bandits. She's married to Ben. She is short, spunky and a lot of fun to be around. When we get the chance to talk, it's always enlightening and enjoyable. I haven't seen her since I got back to Merced, but I plan to frequent CB in the coming months, so I hope to see her and talk. She has a penchant for changing her hairstyle. When I first met her, she had a shaved head. Now she has shaved sides on her head, and a tousle of dark blonde hair on the top of her head.

Patrick. He's a lot of fun. He's really talented. He acts for a living and is very good at what he does. I met him through Sophie. He's a little taller than me, with a completely shaved head, a beard and has large holes in his ears. We talk about art and writing and films. He's about to make it big in the film industry, and I am very happy for him. We smoke together usually in the late evenings, when the air is crisp (as it's still winter here) and the spotlight highlights the smoke we smoke. We are going to collaborate on making scripts for short films, and also produce them. I have never written a screenplay, so it will be neat to try something new writing-wise.

Sophie is an artist. She is also a feminist. She's super smart and really nice. I met her at Coffee Bandits. We usually (but not lately) get together once a week and collaborate. She paints a painting, and I write a poem to her painting. Sometimes we do 4 poems/paintings, or sometimes only one. She's really great to talk to, and I enjoy her company.

Michael is Sophie's boyfriend. He's half African American and half Chicano. He's well-built and he makes me laugh a lot. He's a musician. He plays the guitar. And he's a good musician too. I've witnessed him playing his guitar and it sounds so good.

Will is a herb enthusiast. He lives across the street from me. He grows plants. Fruits, aloe vera, and other plants. He's mellow and talks softly. When Sophie was living at the house I live at now, he would come over to drink beers and smoke pot with us. He's a hard worker and a good friend.

Dob. The Artist. A talented and devoted one at that. He lives a few houses away from my house. He has long, curly, greying hair, wears glasses, and enjoys drinking rum. When I go over to his house, we sit and talk about art and politics. He wants me to document his life story. We are also going to promote each other. He with his art, me with my poetry collections and essay/story collections.

There are a few others, but they don't live here in Merced. There's Jordan, and he's a cool guy who does lots of different artistic things. His wife Alison is a musician/artist/poet.

Cariss is one of two roommates that I am living with. She's a thin, blonde haired woman. She's originally from Merced, but she lived in various parts of California for the past few years. She and I are buddies. We talk all the time and she's really cool to be around.

Sal is my other roommate. He's very tall, and very kind. He speaks fast and we get along well. He takes care of the bills for the house, and he also drives me to the market when I want to get groceries. He also takes me to other places, when he has the time. He took me to the train station, and he also took me to my doctor's appointment. I like Sal. He's a good roommate and we don't chat often, but when we do, it's cordial and polite.

The wonderful thing about most of these friends, and I have mentioned it already with a couple of them, is they like to smoke pot. It's 420 friendly where I go to when I meet my friends. I have eliminated almost every stimulant in my life. Mostly because I feel a lot better without them. So no alcohol, no pot. I do smoke. And I do drink caffeine. I guess those things are stimulants. But I've eliminated the big ones.

Tomorrow, I'll write about my life here in Merced.

So here's what I usually do during the weekdays and weekends.

First of all I sleep badly. I wake up 4-5 times a night, and sometimes stay up after I've woken up for a while. I take sleeping pills, but they mostly don't help. I usually get up around 5 am and check my emails and Facebook. Then I'll either take my caffeine pills or go back to sleep. Then, after waking up at around 7-7:30, I'll get up for the day.

Around 8 or so, I'll go over to Dob's house. We drink coffee, talk and we discuss about how to further each other's careers. His, his art career, me, my writing career. I'll stay for 3-4 hours and then I head back home.

Before I go into my house, I check the mail. Most times there isn't anything for me, but when I make an order to Amazon at the beginning of the month, I do get packages. Right now I'll be getting 5 packages in the mail in the coming days.

I take a 2-3 hour nap. It helps recharge my batteries and it feels good to rest.

Around 1 pm, I'll start reading my books. I have 5 piles of books. Writing, writing related, novels, poetry related, and poetry books. I'll read for about 3 hours. It takes that long to get through all the piles.

Back on the computer, and I check emails and surf the net. I am on Facebook constantly, and I enjoy reading my newsfeed. Then occasionally, I'll read some articles online.

By 5 pm, I'm getting a little hungry. So I get something to eat. Usually oats and water. Then back on the computer.

At around 7:30, I write. That goes between 20-30 minutes. It just depends on what I'm writing. I take longer when I write prose, shorter when I write poetry.

After writing, I'll watch a movie, TV show, or video. I am a connoisseur of poetry and writing related DVDs. I have 3 different series of poetry DVDs, and I also have a few movies with writing, writers, poetry and/or poets in my collection. Sometimes I'll watch a comedy or drama based movie.

I read a little more. These books are poets/writers interviews books. After that, I read some of my writing magazines.

Finally, I hit the sack around 11-11:30 pm. Sometimes Patrick comes over to smoke and talk. I'll be up a little later if he does come over.

What I do constantly during the day and night- I smoke my pipe, I listen to various bands and genres of music, and I drink a lot of water.

So that's what I do during the weekdays.

On the weekends, I'm mostly on the computer. I'm on Facebook, Twitter and my email. I read a little, mostly my magazines. And if there's a sports event on the TV, I'll watch that. On Sunday nights, there is this HBO show called 'Girls'. It's about these people that live in NYC and their lives. One girl, the main character, is a writer. They show a lot of nudity, and some cussing. But it's interesting. I'm going to start watching a Showtime show called 'Californication'. It's about a writer who is blocked.

So that's my life in a nutshell. Tomorrow, my thoughts on writing and my philosophy and so forth.

My writing process is fairly simple and easy. I used to have a lot of prepping to do before I wrote, but now I have narrowed it down to just a couple of things.

First, I have to smoke immediately before I write. The high of nicotine gives me a boost and it makes me relax. Second, I put on some music. Right now it's a slew of pop songs. This also stimulates me and it makes me feel good to hear the music blaring through the speakers. Lastly, I open up the word processor and then start writing. When I write I don't think, I just write. When it comes to poetry, I do try to think of images and scenarios that I can write about. Prose is simpler. I actually think during the day about what I want to write about, and by the time I'm at the laptop ready to write, the information that was gathered during the day from thinking about writing comes to the blank page.

These series of vignettes have come to me easily. I know what I want to write about, and it just comes. When I write, I am in the zone. They call it 'flow'. I'm actually reading a book on writing flow and the words that I read in that book are very familiar.

I believe that writer's block does not exist. I have never had writer's block, but sympathize with those writers that do believe that they have writer's block when they can't manage to write. I take breaks in between writing, usually between 2 weeks and 2 months, depending on what I had been working on. Filling up the well, so to speak.

I read a lot of articles on writing. I am always trying to gain as much knowledge as I can when it concerns writing. Just today I read various writing articles from this online writing magazine called 'Luna Luna'. Good stuff and I learned some new things about poetry and writing.

I am a procrastinator. I always have been. Except when it comes to writing. I always make sure that I write at close to the same time every day, or whatever my writing schedule is. Usually I have been writing every day. When I write my poetry, I write 4 days in a row, and take off 3. For other mundane things, like cleaning my office space in my room, making the bed (I haven't made the bed in years), general cleaning my room, going to the pharmacy to pick up my prescriptions, and all that stuff, I am always at the last moment, last day of the week, or the last minute. But, I'm usually on time when I have appointments. Actually I am usually early. An old habit that has been beneficial for me and whoever I'm seeing.

I am a Democrat. I see a lot of hate for my party online, but the Republican Party has been socially inept for a long time now. They have made many decisions in Congress that has affected me, friends, and people that I know. I'm not a die-hard liberal. I straddle the fence most of the time. But I do lean left.

Everyone should be able to live the life they want to live, within the boundaries of the law. If you want to be a doctor, good for you. If you want to marry and have kids, go for it. If you want to leave the USA and live in Paris, London, Tokyo, etc., then good luck to you. There are still so many stigmas against most people in this country. If you are GLBTQ, the odds are stacked against you. If you are a single mom, it's tough. You want an abortion, well, it's going to be difficult. And many other things and issues. I love my country, but there is so much we need to do to make this country more progressive and better, for all of us, no matter who you are.

I'm an introvert. Well, that's not necessarily the whole truth. When I was younger, I'd be out and about, going to my friends' houses, hanging out at the cafes, and sometimes playing sports. As I got older, I became more closed off. I think that's when my artistic ability came to be. I published my first book in 1999. It was a book of poetry. It sold 52 copies. The people who bought the book told me it was good. Not great, but good. I didn't think much about that. Then I gave a copy of the collection to my therapist. The next week, the first thing she asked was if I was drunk when I wrote it. I hesitantly said yes. I wasn't too sure what to make of her question.

I have been drinking since 15 years old. The first night I drank and got drunk, I was at home at my parent's house and there were a few things that were left over in the refrigerator. A 12 ounce bottle of stout. Some wine coolers, and I think maybe a couple bottles of ale. I drank them alone in my room. Earlier in the evening I had had a triple cheeseburger and fries. After drinking these bottles, I soon got sick. I went to the laundry room sink and threw up. I went to sleep. The next morning, with my head aching, there was a pounding on my door. I opened it and it was my dad. He asked me if I had thrown up in the laundry room sink. I said yes. He knew I had been drinking. He told me to clean up the mess, and that we wouldn't tell my mom.

When I turned 21, it was even worse. I'd get drunk after work with my friend, who worked at a bar/restaurant. He would bring six-packs of beer and he also had hard alcohol. We'd drink to grunge era songs and we'd always end up passed out on his two beds. Later in life, I'd be on and off drinking. Now, in the present, I do not drink anymore. It must have been interesting to my best friend, who has drunk sparingly in his life, to see us drunk. Now I am the observer. I don't miss it at all. I don't know if I'd be classified as an alcoholic or a recovering one. But one thing's for sure, I will never touch another drop.

Back to the introvert subject. I'd stayed in my parent's house, housebound, for two years straight. I had been diagnosed as anxiety-prone, as well as agoraphobic. I saw my first therapist at the age of

25. Then on and off from jobs and therapists. And now I am mostly in my room. I think I mentioned this already. I take medicine for my mental illnesses. And for the most part they do work. I do suffer another mental illness, and I'll go more into that tomorrow.

I suffer from schizophrenia. I have had this mental illness since 2002. It first happened in Texas. I went to Fort Worth to live with a friend. Needless to say, it was a bad move on my part. Near the end of my stay there, I started to hear voices. I wasn't sure if they were real or not, but I found out, by listening closely, that they were indeed not real. I talked to my sister on the phone and told her that I was hearing voices. She promptly told my dad, and got me on the first plane back to California.

I entered the psychiatric ward a week later. I was there for 2 weeks. I was very unhappy there, but knew that the doctors and nurses were there to help me. I took some medicines and it helped. When I was released, I went back to my parent's house to live. I gained a lot of weight due to the medication's side effects. I slept most of the time and watched television. But my parents were sympathetic and let me live life like that.

I was alright for a few months. Then I decided to save up the money that I was getting from public assistance, and bought a ticket to London. I wanted to go back and see all of my old haunts. Oh, I lived in London for 6 months when I was 22. That is where I met Tiffany. More on her later. I had a great life when I lived there. But my visa ran out and I had to go back to America.

So I ended up back in London. Then I went to Valencia, Spain. I was off my medications. I started to hear voices again. I called from a dingy payphone on the streets of Valencia and talked to my mom. She got me a job with my aunt in Hawaii. So I went there.

While in Hawaii, I worked in my aunt's office. She's an oncologist. I started seeing a psychologist and a psychiatrist. I was back on meds. After 8 months, I wanted to go back to Europe. I bought a one-way ticket to Paris. My aunt told my mom of my plans, and my mom vehemently told me not to go. She offered me the chance to go back home. I decided that I wanted to be with my family. So I went back.

I was alright for a couple months. Then I went off my meds again, hoping that I'd be alright. Nope. The voices came back. I was slated to start an outpatient program at a nearby hospital. Then the night before I was supposed to start the program, I heard the worst voices of all. They said I was going to die and it would be horrible. So instead, I took all the pills I had been saving from my meds, and swallowed all 30 of them. I closed my eyes and went to sleep.

When I woke up the next morning, I couldn't speak. My vision was blurred and it was difficult to stand. My mom was home still and she saw what kind of state I was in. She had to help me to the car as I wobbled down the walkway. She took me to the ER. They gave me a liquid charcoal drink to clean out my system. They admitted me into the psychiatric ward, my second trip there. The drugs didn't wear off until the next day.

I stayed there for 2 weeks, just like before. I got bored and it was not fun at all. My mom came and visited every day. I got to see my nephew and sisters on Halloween.

I've since been in the psychiatric ward 5 times. For the same symptoms of schizophrenia. The anxiety does come too, sometimes. I am taking a couple of medications. I still hear voices now and then, so I'm not completely cured. I can't concentrate or focus when I do hear the voices. This is something that will most likely be with me for the rest of my life.

Next up- sleep patterns.

I haven't slept through the night in, I can't remember when. This has been a regular occurrence for 15 years. When I was a teenager and young adult, I would sleep through the night easily. And for at least 10 hours. Now, I am resigned to the fact that I will never sleep through the night ever again.

I usually get up 4-5 times a night. I think I mentioned this earlier. I get up most times, just get up and smoke. I'm groggy and sometimes I can't focus in my right eye. Then I'll go to the bathroom or surf the net on the computer. By then I'm tired enough to go back to sleep.

I take a lot of naps. Probably 3 or 4 a day. For 2 hours at a time. I'm really ready to go in the early evening. I take my meds after I've eaten, as I suffer from side effects if I don't eat first.

I drool a lot on my pillow. And my long hair gets in it. Definitely disgusting. I sometimes find myself rolling left to right, right to left. My dreams lately have been really strange. I've dreamt about being at my former workplace more than a few times. Sometimes I dream that I'm playing baseball or soccer. I played both sports from a young age through high school. One time I dreamed about my grandma when she was a child. She was on the carousel eating cotton candy. Another dream was when I was swimming and I dropped to the bottom. I remember waking up and not being able to breathe.

Tiffany. Ah yes.

Tiffany Silverman was a 19 year old teenager when I met her. We met through her brother, who, with he, his girlfriend and Tiffany, were in London, England for the summer to work. I met her on a warm sultry night, and I saw her in the lobby of the hotel I was staying at, at the beginning of my stay. She was beautiful. She had long red hair, doe-brown eyes and a full pair of lips. I was instantly smitten. We got to know each other after a couple of weeks. I stayed at her flat for days at a time. We were never officially a couple, but we were for sure more than friends. She left at the end of summer, and I have been missing her from that day on.

I have old pictures of her with me when we were in London. And with the advent of Facebook, I am her friend there. I see what she looks like now. Not much has changed. But she does look a little older. I love her. I have for the longest time. Let's just say years. I never told her that I loved her when we were there together in London. But I've carried her in my heart all these years.

I can go on with the heartaches and heartbreaks, but I'm sure you have heard it all before. All I'll say is this. Dearest Tiffany, you are the Love Of My Life. You have been, you are, and you always will be.

If you get a chance, in 2016 my memoir of when I lived in London will be published. The title of the book is; My Time In London : Six Months In The City Of Dreams. (Insert shameless plug here.)

My friend and confidant Jim Pacelli and I have been friends for over 25 years. We have both fulfilled our lifelong dreams of living abroad, we both have had bad breakups, and we've drank and sang and laughed together for many, many nights. Now I live here in Merced, and he lives in Sunnyvale, which is a suburb of San Jose.

We talk on the phone once a week or every other week. He's a great friend. We talk about sports, his work at the Fillmore in San Francisco, and my writing. I haven't seen him for 6 months now. He's a very likable person. Mellow and sympathetic. He's 5'8, lanky, brown eyes and black hair. He used to have a mustache when he was younger, but has been clean shaven for a long time now.

We went to Big Sur one weekend a long time ago. He had just broken up with his girlfriend of 3 years. We saw some amazing things there. Many redwoods. A hidden cove. A forest with laughing water. It was heavenly.

So, I'll see Jim in a couple of months. We'll go to coffee or maybe lunch and coffee. We'll talk and hang out. Miss you, my friend.

I think we should treat everyone equally. There are so many people that live here on planet earth, and we seem to be slipping into a kind of melancholy. We don't say hi to strangers on the street. We don't say thank you to the understaffed coffee shop employee. And we always seem to be negative. Alright, I understand that the world we live in is not the best of places to live. But if we were more kind to each other, more happy, more into making this world a better place, I think that would be something extraordinary.

The television is definitely a negative influence on our culture. I mean, there are good things about it, but if you are like me, I see negative in it. The news. Always so negative. There are wars, there are horrible things that people do to each other, and to animals. There is a lot of suffering and neglect. I can't fathom how it would be if I lived in a third world country, or if I was really wound up about life. I see people stare with venom in their eyes at others. Money is king. When you don't have money, you want it. Badly. I don't watch television for the news anymore. Only for sports.

The Internet can be bad or good. I've noticed both. On Facebook, there are good things happening to people, and other people congratulating them. I have some good friends on Facebook. But I spend too much time on it. That's the gaffe. Our time is so wrapped up on media and the Internet. Before the Internet, I'd go over to my friends' houses and hang out, play, have a good time. Now kids are playing video games, watching videos online, and so forth.

The solution? To change our way of thinking. To eliminate negative thinking and jaded thinking and to be positive. I do my best to be as good to everyone as I can. No matter if they treat me badly or with mean intentions. I, myself, am not the sole solution. But I believe if people were like me, positive and happy and living life with intention, life would be better, not for only them, but for everyone. My 2 cents.

Letters

Dearest Tiffany,

I know you haven't heard from me in a long time. That doesn't mean I haven't thought of you. I have thought of you every day, a lot. I still love you. I have always loved you. I know that you have been disappointed with me because throughout my absence in your life, starting from the day you left for home from London until now, it has been difficult. And with many problems you have faced. I have a picture of you on my desk, with you smiling. It looks like you are really happy. I hope you were happy too, when I was in your life.

Things here are going well. I want you to come visit me. I have been writing and enjoying the California weather. It was 72 today. I looked at the newspaper and saw that Montreal was in the freezing temps. The sun would do you good, and if you do come, we could do all the things we always wanted to do together.

I cry sometimes. When in bed, hoping to roll over and see you next to me. I miss talking to you. Remember all those late nights when we would just talk? We have memories together, and it would be nice to reminisce. Perhaps you don't wish to come. That is okay too.

The day will come, someday, when we will be able to walk on the beach, hold hands, and feel each other's warmth and love. I hold on to that thought and ask God to grant me this one wish.

Okay, I hope all is well, and that you are healthy, happy and living the life you have always wanted, Take care.

Love Always,

Steve

To My Neighbor,

I don't think I can hold it in any longer. Please refrain from dancing naked in front of your living room window. It frightens me and the neighbors as well. I'm sure you have some perfectly sane explanation why you do that, but it won't go well with my wife. She says that you are going to make the neighbors sign a petition to get you evicted.

I am a simple man with simple wants and needs. But seeing you naked is not one of them. I am not going to berate you for your oversized stomach, red face with a smile on those thin lips of yours, nor for the horrendous dancing you do. But please put on some clothes from now on.

Another thing. Your tangerines are falling on my lawn. Suffice it to say, it reminds me of your testicles. They are falling at a rate of 5 per day, and soon my lawn will look like one of those barrels with water and apples. You know, like bobbing for apples? But instead, bobbing for your testicles.

Last, but not least, I know you like to flirt with the mail woman when she comes to deliver your mail. She has told me that every time she sees you, she cringes. It's not the patches of beard on your face that scares her. It's the way you talk. She says you sound like a razor cutting on stone. And she doesn't like your scent. She says you smell like a silent-but-deadly fart had gone off.

So here's the summary of what I'd like you to not do from now on. 1. Don't dance naked in front of your window. 2. Pick up your tangerines from our lawn, or cut some of the branches off. 3. No flirting with the mail woman. Okay. I hope this letter has been clear to you. Have a nice day, and my wife says that she'll try and drop by soon to make you a tangerine pie.

Sincerely,

John Smith, your next door neighbor.

Dear Lance,

How's it going? I hope all is well with you, my friend. We haven't talked or met for lunch for a long time now, and I apologize. Since we live in different cities now, it is difficult to come see you. As for not calling you, you know I am always busy writing or doing something in the writing business. But I hope to see you soon.

The reason I'm writing is because I feel guilty. I know when we were growing up together, I wasn't the best of friends. I called you names and treated you like crap. I want to take the time out now, and say, I'm sorry. I'm sorry for all of that. I was a mean kid and I guess maybe the things going on in my home was indicative of what my meanness towards you was. I'm not making excuses. That's the last thing I want to do. But I think saying I'm sorry is what I can do now, since I am an adult, and I want to confront my childhood.

We had some great times when we were kids, though, right? I remember us writing our stories and novels in Mr. Kage's class and playing Dungeons and Dragons with Pat, Stu, Shawn and the rest of them. I remember the time when I came over to your house in the early morning, 5 am, I think, and we watched the space shuttle go up into space. Lugging all our D&D stuff to class in that red tote. I forgot the name that was on that bag, but I'm sure you do remember. I have this one memory when we were is class, and Mr. Kage was picking names for softball teams for P.E. When I noticed that you weren't on my team, I felt like crying.

We are brothers, you and I. We've been through a few things together, and it has been a pleasure having you as my friend. We shall continue that friendship until the day we die. I'll phone you soon.

Your Best Friend,

Steve

To The Angry Man At The Restaurant,

You were very rude. You have no right to yell and scream and act like a spoiled child. You made the server cry, and that is unforgivable.

So what, your steak was well-done instead of medium rare? You were ordering drinks left and right. The server was too busy, but she accommodated you anyway. She brought your drinks promptly. You drank them quickly. What was it? Whiskey? And then the bottle of red wine.

You must be lonely, or very, very angry. Is it your life at home? Maybe your wife is cheating on you. Maybe your house is up for foreclosure. I don't exactly know.

So you made the server cry. Are you happy now? I'm sure, in your smug little way, you feel satisfied with your tantrums and immature behavior. I think it's time for you to leave.

I think you need to think more about others than of your own pathetic self. There are people who are way worse off than you. A lot worse. How would you like it if you lived somewhere where you couldn't have fresh, clean water? That is given to you, free of charge, when you sat down at your table. What about food? There are millions, and children are most of them, who are starving. Yes, you have money in your pocket. You drive a car. Maybe not the best model, but you don't have to walk or take the bus. You have a roof over your head. What the hell?

You should apologize to the server. If I were not a pacifist, I'd grab your arm and march you to the register so you can say, "I'm very, very sorry for my behavior. Here's a 30% tip for your troubles." Of course you won't do this. But, remember, karma.

Sincerely,

An Offended Diner

Dear Dad,

I know we haven't had the most close of relationships, but I know we are getting closer. We talk more than we used to, you are starting to give me advice again. I guess we both aren't getting younger, so time goes by and if we don't take advantage of it, we'll grow old and then die, without letting each other know that we love each other.

You're retired now, after a long career. Now you get to relax and enjoy life, as you had when you were a younger person in love with life. I know when I was born, you were so happy. You were always there for me and my sisters. You worked hard and had food on the table, a roof over our heads. And clothes to wear. I will always be grateful for your sacrifices.

We don't hug or touch. But I remember two times when we did. The first time was when you were coaching at baseball. I tripped and fell while walking to the dugout. You thought I was just lazing around. You yelled at me in front of all the players and their dads. Then someone told you I had tripped. After everyone left practice, you apologized and hugged me.

The second time was when you went in for surgery for your heart. You had just gotten out of surgery. I, in a fit of love, put my hand in yours. Even in your incapacitated state, you had the strength to squeeze it. I almost had tears in my eyes.

Okay, Dad, I'll make you a promise. I'll always love you, and we'll have our disagreements, but I'll be there for you for anything. Anything.

Love your only son,

Steve

Dear Young Boy In The Toy Store,

I know you don't get to come here often. If at all. Your clothes are dirty and tattered. I see your shoes are worn out. Your face has a couple of smudges of dirt on it. I wonder where you are from. You look at the toys. I see a gleam in your eyes. Maybe you're hoping to get one of the toys you've been looking at for so long. I know you don't have any money to able to buy one, but just looking makes you feel happy.

A woman and her son push you aside so they can get the toy you have been eyeing. They try to be nice, but they are rude. I grimace as you turn your face downward. I wonder if you will cry. You wipe a few tears from your eyes.

I say enough is enough. I walk up to you and pick the toy up from the shelf. "This one?" I ask you. You nod shyly. I tell you to follow me to the front of the store.

I pay for the toy and give you the bag. You smile with your toothy smile, and my heart leaps in my chest. I tousle your unkempt brown hair and say goodbye. You suddenly grab me by the hand and lead me outside.

I see an elderly man sitting on the ground. He is very dirty and smells like the garbage cans that are nearby. He points to you and you sit down next to him. I smile at the elderly man and pull a few bills out of my pocket. I give them to him.

The elderly man has a gleam in his eye. He shakes my hand and thanks me. Not so much for the toy or the money, but that I brought joy to his young son. I say goodbye to both of you and walk back to my car. Take care, both of you. You will both be in my prayers tonight.

Glad I Could Help,

A friend for life

Dear Facebook,

I love you and I hate you.

You give me a community of people whom I can love and trust. You give me happiness when someone has something great in their life to say. For example. A writer I know on Facebook has gotten into a wonderful relationship with a man. She is very happy and she really enjoys being with him. She had been single for a time and she was, well, I won't say miserable, but missing someone in her life. And now she has it.

You make me spend too much time on you. I'm always reading a lot of different posts on my friends. You have a newsfeed, which I was trying to avoid. News makes me sad, especially negative news. I don't want to see that.

You make me communicate with people. I have friends in real life, but not many. You help me get through my social anxiety and put me in contact with the world-at-large. I am grateful to be friends with artists, writers, poets, musicians, actors, hard-working people, and all the other people I am in contact with.

You make me feel like I don't have a life. I'm liking statuses and writing comments. It's fun, but I'm not getting any better socially. You let me feel like I don't matter when someone doesn't like my posts, or doesn't comment on my posts.

You show me that we, as humans, can find a like-minded place together and share our lives to each other. I like that most of all about you. You show me that I can meet people, whether that is online, or in person after meeting someone online.

All in all, I have to say I'm grateful for your presence. The good outweighs the bad, though I will still complain about the newsfeed with the news on it. I do come across some strange and crazy people on you, but that's alright, as I am strange and crazy too. So, thank you. Or maybe no thank you.

Sincerely,

A Person Who Loves And Hates You

Steve Baba is a writer and poet living in Merced, California. He has lived in many different places in the USA. He loves reading, meeting up with his artist friends for a nice chat, and hanging out at the coffee shops gossiping and talking about everything about life. Hit On The Head With A Sledgehammer is his 2nd collection of writings. Currently writing his memoir on the time he lived in London, Steve is all left-handed and a product of bad grades in high school and a broken career as a college student.

www.ingramcontent.com/pod-product-compliance
Lightning Source LLC
Chambersburg PA
CBHW060823120626
46557CB00001B/341